"If you've just learned that someone you love has cancer, you're holding the perfect 'What can I do?' book. *Caring for a Loved One with Cancer* is filled with countless practical pointers that could only be compiled by someone who has been there. A must-have for caregivers and patients alike."

> **Otis W. Brawley,** MD, Chief Medical Officer, National Home Office, American Cancer Society

"June triumphs over her trials by sharing with caregivers scores of time-tested tips and to-dos that made a definitive difference in her successful struggle. This book will truly help you help others."

> **Joel T. Allison,** President & CEO, Baylor Health Care System

"An excellent book . . . a great resource with truly practical tips for helping friends or loved ones live with cancer. It should be in every home."

> **Joe McIlhaney Jr.,** MD, Founder & Chairman, The Medical Institute

"Could only have been written by one who has personally experienced this 'unfriendly foe.' As a breast cancer survivor/conqueror, I found the advice on how to minister to the children of cancer patients to be especially caring and valuable."

> **Merry Nell Drummond,** Cofounder, Austin, TX, chapter of Bosom Buddies

"Focused on the medical aspects of cancer care, I often forget the integral role friends and family play in patient recovery. With this book, June reinforces invaluable, practical actions we should never forget, and shows how to share God's love with cancer patients."

> **Roberto Rodriguez Ruesga,** MD, FACS, FASCRS, Colorectal Surgeon

"There is an art to walking with others wounded by illness. June's practical book equips all willing souls to turn our efforts into a masterpiece. Read . . . walk . . . and be blessed."

> **Adam L. Myers,** M.D., CHCQM, CPHRM, Senior Vice President, Chief Medical Officer, Methodist Health System

"As a cancer survivor and program manager at a cancer center, I come in contact with a lot of material related to the cancer experience. It is so refreshing to find such valuable information written with the loved ones of cancer patients in mind. I would strongly recommend this book, not only for anyone who knows someone diagnosed with cancer, but also for cancer treatment centers."

Janet Kirklen, RN, Program Manager/Nurse Educator,
Baylor Charles A. Sammons Cancer Center

"Having worked with many cancer patients over the past fifty years, I know how important is the support of family and friends. Such support can result in prolongation of life and certainly its quality. June does a wonderful job answering the questions asked by family members. This book is a classic."

Kenneth H. Cooper, MD, MPH, Founder and Chairman,
Cooper Aerobics Center

CARING

for a LOVED ONE *with*

CANCER

Other Crossway Books by June Hunt:

Hope for Your Heart: Finding Strength in Life's Storms
Bonding with Your Teen through Boundaries

CARING
for a LOVED ONE *with*
CANCER

JUNE HUNT

:: CROSSWAY

WHEATON, ILLINOIS

Caring for a Loved One with Cancer

Copyright © 2011 by Hope for the Heart, Inc.

Published by Crossway
        1300 Crescent Street
        Wheaton, Illinois 60187

The material presented in this book is not intended to and does not provide nor should be construed to provide medical advice or consultation, but rather offers information for greater understanding of the human condition, spirituality, and interpersonal relationships that may sometimes be affected by biochemical or physiological conditions or diagnoses such as cancer. Consult with a qualified caregiver regarding any medical questions, diagnoses, or treatments.

Cover design: Brand Navigation

Cover image: Masterfile

First printing 2011

Printed in the United States of America

Unless otherwise indicated, Scripture quotations are from the HOLY BIBLE, NEW INTERNATIONAL VERSION®. Copyright © 1973, 1978, 1984 Biblica. Used by permission of Zondervan. All rights reserved. The "NIV" and "New International Version" trademarks are registered in the United States Patent and Trademark Office by Biblica. Use of either trademark requires the permission of Biblica.

Scripture quotations marked ESV are from the ESV® Bible (*The Holy Bible, English Standard Version®*), copyright © 2001 by Crossway Bibles. Used by permission. All rights reserved.

Scripture quotations marked KJV are from the *King James Version* of the Bible.

Scripture quotations marked MESSAGE are from *The Message*. Copyright © by Eugene H. Peterson 1993, 1994, 1995, 1996, 2000, 2001, 2002. Used by permission of NavPress Publishing Group.

Scripture references marked NKJV are from The New King James Version. Copyright © 1982, Thomas Nelson, Inc. Used by permission.

Trade paperback ISBN: 978-1-4335-2707-4
PDF ISBN: 978-1-4335-2708-1
Mobipocket ISBN: 978-1-4335-2709-8
ePub ISBN: 978-1-4335-2710-4

Library of Congress Cataloging-in-Publication Data
Hunt, June.
   Caring for a loved one with cancer / June Hunt.
      p. cm.
   Includes bibliographical references (p. 109).
   ISBN 978-1-435-2707-4 (tp)
   1. Caregivers—Religious life. 2. Cancer—Patients—Care.
3. Cancer—Religious aspects—Christianity. I. Title.
BV4910.33.H86   2011
248.8'6196994—dc22   2011017073

Crossway is a publishing ministry of Good News Publishers.

VP		21	20	19	18	17	16	15	14	13	12	11
14	13	12	11	10	9	8	7	6	5	4	3	2	1

To the Memory
of
Charles Ansbacher

my brother-in-law, whose courageous battle against
brain cancer ended September 12, 2010—almost
thirteen months after his initial diagnosis,
with abiding admiration.

During my own battle with cancer—after I had lost my
hair and was trying to get used to wigs and hats—Charles
(and my sister Swanee) didn't want me to feel alone in the
hat department. So Charles brought unique encouragement
to me by wearing a "Goofy" hat all evening. Needless to
say, the "Goofy photo" on page 57 belied his reputation as
a world-renowned symphony conductor. The caring heart
that inspired his gift of encouragement to me also guided his
musical gift of encouragement to the world.

For twenty years, Charles conducted the Colorado
Springs Symphony. After strategizing to create the Pikes
Peak Center for the Performing Arts—renowned for unparal-
leled acoustics—Charles was inducted into the White House
Fellows program. He then served as director of artistic design
for the new Denver International Airport.

In 1993, after my sister Swanee was appointed US ambas-
sador to Austria, Charles found himself in a musical paradise.
"Unpacking his baton, he used the opportunity to carry musical inspiration from his new base in Vienna"[1] and became a
"true hero for the people of Sarajevo, and of all Bosnia,"[2]
revitalizing a "decimated Philharmonic"[3] in a city belea-
guered by a three–year siege and traumatized by genocide.

Following their return to the United States, Charles
founded the Boston Landmarks Orchestra, which he conducted for ten years—providing outdoor symphonic music
(in the Arthur Fiedler tradition) free of charge at numerous
well-known landmarks throughout the city.

Yet reality lets us know that in the concert of life, no one gets a program. Thus, in the first month after his diagnosis, Charles and Swanee set forth these inspiring guidelines: "We *hope* for twenty years, *plan* for eighteen months, *prepare* for death today, and *treasure* each moment . . . *now*."

In midsummer 2010, Charles began receiving hospice care. Undeterred, he maintained a strong hand in leading the orchestra and became the first conductor to hold a symphonic concert at Fenway Park and the first to lead an orchestra while in hospice.

Just eleven days before his death, I joined a handful of family members and close friends (along with seven thousand other enthusiastic fans) at Boston's Hatch Shell to attend what would be his final concert. At age sixty-seven, after more than fifty years of conducting in more than forty countries, Charles and his baton were laid to rest in Boston . . . but the memory of this remarkable man and his rapturous music will live forever in my heart.

June

June and Charles

CONTENTS

PART TWO

Help and Hope

ACKNOWLEDGMENTS

Writing *Caring for a Loved One with Cancer* was not unlike conducting a symphony with various key players entering and exiting on cue to perform a masterpiece. So, with deepest gratitude I sincerely thank . . .

Dr. Joyce O'Shaughnessy, who not only directed me throughout my cancer journey, but who also made additional manuscript edits that were music to my ears.

Barbara Spruill, Kay Deakins, and **June Page,** who recorded many notes that were "musts" for the manuscript.

Connie Steindorf and **Beth Stapleton,** who played key reading roles, never missing a beat.

Syl Mallette, whose original page design—along with **Josh Dennis's** cover—scaled the heights of excellence.

Angie White, who harmonized production deadlines . . . while **Josh Armstrong** composed new photos.

Phillip Bleecker, who sounded the opening notes on the index . . . and closing notes on proofing along with **Karen Williams.**

Bea Garner, who reviewed scores of copy to ensure accuracy. And **Jill Prohaska** and **Eula Scott,** who chimed in beautifully at the end.

Elizabeth Cunningham, who didn't stop beating the drum until the last notes were added.

Friends and **family,** whose loving care and concern carried the melody heard through all the pages of this book.

The **Orchestrator** of my life, who shepherded me through the "valley of the shadow" and put a song in my heart and gave me a story to share.

"Because you are my help, I sing in the shadow of your wings."
PSALM 63:7

Dear Friend,

What can you do when someone receives a devastating diagnosis? Do you have difficulty communicating your love and concern? Is there anything you can do to make a *real* difference?

Sometimes we don't know how to show we care. Sometimes we don't know how to express our concern. Sometimes we don't know what others need from us.

During my own bout with cancer, my friends and family were absolutely extraordinary. Countless people ministered to me during my battle with cancer. The Lord knows who they are and how grateful I am for each and every one. Though I don't identify all of them in terms of their relationship to me, I mention their first names in the pages that follow to recognize them and let them know that their ministry of love still lives on in my heart. That's why I want to share the specific acts of love they performed that helped me face this unfriendly foe—*the many deeds that made a real difference.*

My prayer is that this practical little book will help you express your heart and extend your care to any and every loved one who comes face-to-face with cancer or any critical illness.

Yours in the Lord's peace,
June Hunt

"The wise in heart are called discerning,
and pleasant words promote instruction."
PROVERBS 16:21

INTRODUCTION

"You do have cancer. You will have a mastectomy. You will lose your hair." The radiologist delivered these exact words so matter-of-factly. I sat on the examining table that Tuesday afternoon—absolutely stunned.

What does my hair have to do with this? was my first thought. Then my mind quickly raced in another direction. *But . . . on Friday I have to lead a three-day conference in Baltimore . . . then next Monday I must be in New York City. I don't have time for surgery!*

Please understand, in 2001 my diagnosis came like an ambush, just one month after the 9/11 terrorist attacks on United States soil at the hands of Islamic extremists. Two hijacked planes torpedoed the World Trade Center; the Twin Towers imploded; a third plane plowed into the Pentagon; a fourth plane targeted the White House, but a handful of passengers—American heroes—foiled that plot and all passengers died on an empty Pennsylvania field, not on Pennsylvania Avenue in Washington DC.

That morning, nearly three thousand people lost their lives in the startling attack that shocked the world. As captured on camera, horrified witnesses saw men and women jumping from high windows to their deaths, innocent lives snuffed out, others crushed beneath tons of cement and steel. Immediately, our country went into mourning on a monumental scale.

Personally I had never seen such outpouring of grief—shared grief—week after week after week. While dark clouds hovered over America like a shroud, New Yorkers especially were trying to feel their way through a thick fog of agony, turmoil, and anguish. Despite the threat of my own personal physical implosion, *not going* to New York was not an option. The American Association of Christian Counselors (AACC) had requested that I come to speak at their "Trauma and Grief" conference—not to counsel 9/11 victims but to offer counsel to those counseling the victims. (Hundreds of counselors, pastors, and other leaders were asking for help, and I felt deeply humbled *just to be asked* to be of service, and I was genuinely grateful to God for the opportunity to speak on "Crisis Counseling" along with doing personal one-on-one counseling.)

In a strange sense, I felt I could relate to victims of 9/11 on two levels: First, as a horrified unsuspecting citizen who had just been blindsided by traumatic news, and second, as a reeling victim of an enemy attack that might just kill me. Cancer had become *my* silent terrorist. My personal ambush didn't stop with my radiologist's original pronouncement. On Thursday, as I waited to board a plane for Baltimore, my surgeon called to confirm the result of the biopsy. "Yes, you do have a malignancy on the right side," he said, reiterating the radiologist's findings. Dr. Jones, however, then unveiled phase two of the ambush: I also had a different, even more aggressive type of cancer growing on the *left* side that was previously undetected because it was growing toward the chest wall. Thus, in a matter of two days I found myself facing bilateral surgery, chemotherapy, radiation, and the prospect of multiple medications for years to come. My life was about to change—*forever*.

Even so, as I reflect back on my earliest thoughts—while still on the examination table—I see how God's Word began ministering to me. Almost instantly, I found myself focused on Philippians 1:20 (ESV), that "Christ will be honored in my body, whether by life or by death." This Scripture became my deep desire, my very personal prayer: "Whether my time is long or whether it is short, may Christ be honored in my body." Though I'd taught through the book of Philippians twice, never before had I focused on this verse. But when life and death were very much in question, this precious passage kept my battle with cancer in focus and literally protected me from experiencing fear. (In truth, I'm amazed that the entire time I never experienced fear!)

King David said, "All the days ordained for me were written in your book before one of them came to be."[4] Likewise, I knew all my days were known and numbered by God. The length of my life was already a settled reality. Although I could not extend my appointed days, I knew I could trust my future to the Lord—no matter the outcome.

Herein lies a profound truth that every cancer victim must grasp: Cancer is never sovereign over anyone's life—only God is. Though I made decisions that influenced my health and well-being, I knew my life was ultimately in His hands. Long ago, I learned that, as a follower of Jesus, nothing can come into my life that hasn't first passed through the heavenly Father's fingers of love. *Nothing.* So I realized that whatever the physical challenge, there would be purpose in the pain and God's grace to get me through it.

On each step of this "fascinating journey," as I came to call it, I've had hope for my heart. Hope is a powerful medicine because it doesn't depend on what doctors diagnose, what test results indicate, or what tangible symptoms suggest. It is rooted in God Himself and what He has specifically promised. A full dose of hope fixes our spiritual eyes on our all-wise, all-powerful, all-loving Lord.[5]

No one welcomes illness on the walk of life; no one enjoys pain as a partner. Personally, I would never have signed up for cancer. If, however, you could somehow roll back the hands of time and stop cancer from intersecting my life's path, I would say, "No!" That path of pain has proven priceless because the compassion I "caught" could have come to me in no other way. Oh, the sensitivity I acquired, the growth I gained, the lessons I learned have been invaluable!

While in New York, I never mentioned my own impending physical implosion—the New Yorkers had as much trauma as they could bear. But after I returned to Dallas, I mentioned my diagnosis during my live two-hour call-in counseling program, HOPE IN THE NIGHT—and that's when the floodgates opened! People began pouring out their own painful stories, their challenging questions, their personal heartaches. Just knowing about my own cancer journey unleashed countless callers reaching out for help and hope. And because I was "walking in their shoes," I earned instant credibility. These strugglers knew I had more than *sympathy*—I had *empathy*; I could identify with them. I had more than *compassion*—I had *connection*; I was "one of them."

During my "fascinating" journey with cancer, my friends and family were absolutely extraordinary. Even now, I'm awed at the many ways they rallied around me, rendering thoughtful acts of loving support that I, myself, could never have imagined.

I also recognize that many cancer sufferers and their physicians don't know what to tell well-intentioned friends and family who earnestly want to provide comfort and care. I know I didn't know either at the time I was diagnosed! This book, *Caring for a Loved One with Cancer*, was born from my sincere desire to pass along the hundreds of real-life, effective, practical helps that made such a dramatic difference in my own life. For me, keeping this information to myself would be unthinkable. I want you and your loved ones to be equally blessed.

My prayer is that this book will help you express your heart and extend your hand to every loved one who comes face-to-face with cancer.

Yours in the Lord's peace,
June Hunt

"Friends love through all kinds of weather,
and families stick together in all kinds of trouble."
PROVERBS 17:17 MESSAGE

PART ONE

Fifty Practical Ways
to Care for Your Loved One

DRIVE YOUR LOVED ONE TO THE DOCTOR— IF CANCER COULD BE THE DIAGNOSIS

Before the C diagnosis (C for cancer), my friend, assistant, and right arm, Kay knew my initial concern. I had a suspicion that a lump might be malignant. Kay said she was going with me for the sonogram. I said, "No, it isn't necessary." She said, "Yes, it is necessary." I said, "No." She said, "Yes!" I said, "No." She said, "Yes." Her persistence won out. And in retrospect, I was glad.

Kay knew that once a doctor gives the cancer diagnosis, the patient remembers only 20 percent of what is subsequently said. Following my examination, the radiologist walked into the room and said, "I'm going to be straightforward with you. You do have cancer. You will have to have a mastectomy. You will have to have chemotherapy. You will lose your hair." (What did hair have to do with this?!)

After telling me I had cancer, the radiologist proceeded to give me all kinds of instructions. But instead of listening, I was thinking, *I can't have surgery right now. I have to speak at a conference in Baltimore in two days and then speak on "Crisis Counseling" in New York City. After all, this is just a month following the September 11, 2001, Islamic terrorist attacks. Our country is in mourning! The doctor needs to understand, I must go.* With my mind whirling so fast, I could hardly hear a word the doctor said. So I interrupted her with my request, "Excuse me, would you please go to the waiting room and ask Kay to join us?"

Kay came in, took notes, and asked questions. Then we both went back to my home office somewhat stunned. How grateful I was to have her there. Throughout my entire ordeal, Kay has lived out the Scripture—again and again—"There is a friend who sticks closer than a brother" (Prov. 18:24 ESV).

And, yes, I was persistent, too. I did lead the conference in Baltimore, and I did speak at the unforgettable conference in New York City.

Don't Withhold Your Tears—
They Tell That Your Heart Is Tender

After hearing the unexpected C news and now back home, we both paused . . . not saying anything.

Finally, I looked at Kay—she had tears in her eyes. Tears. Not her norm. Kay had been tough in public, but now was tender in private. And her tears touched my heart.

Kay encouraged me to call Eleanor. As soon as she heard my voice she asked, "What did the doctor say?" When I told her, she began to sob—loud, heaving sobs. I couldn't believe she was crying for me.

For years Eleanor would say, "I love you," and I believed her. But as she cried, I remember thinking, she *really does love me!*

I was surprised that they were moved to tears. Actually, I was stunned! You see, years ago my father had said—incorrectly, of course—"Tears are a sign of mental illness." So, for years I trained myself not to cry, and even today I'm typically not prone to shed tears.

In truth, I had no idea that the tears of my friends would be so meaningful to me. I knew they stemmed from love. Their tears assured me of their compassion and grounded me in reality. Now I understand the deeper ministry of "weep with those who weep" (Rom. 12:15 NKJV).

I had no idea that the tears of my friends would be so meaningful.
JUNE

Kay showed she cared in many ways, including tears.

3

GATHER A GROUP TO PRAY

My forever friend Barbara immediately called a group of my friends and then let me know that the next evening they were invited to my home for a time of prayer with me. I was really surprised at their immediate response. Then later, prior to each of the two surgeries, they encircled me, each petitioning God on my behalf. Henry led us beautifully, thanking God not only for His sovereign rule over my body and my life, but also for His perfect plan and perfect love for me. Each one asked for my healing but entrusted me to God and to His will rather than to theirs. Following Christ's example, our prayer time concluded with the words: "nevertheless not [our] will, but thine, be done."[6]

I shouldn't have been surprised by their prayerful hearts because the Bible says, "In everything, by prayer and petition, with thanksgiving, present your requests to God. And the peace of God, which transcends all understanding, will guard your hearts and your minds in Christ Jesus" (Phil. 4:6–7). These times of prayer truly provided a precious peace that guarded my heart and guarded my mind.

"The prayer of a righteous man is powerful and effective."
JAMES 5:16

Friends Cheryl, Barbara, Eleanor

25

ᘏ4ᘓ

FOCUS ON FAMILY INVOLVEMENT

The day after my diagnosis, I asked Kay to call my brother, Ray—a very active businessman—to see if he and his wife, Nancy Ann, could come to my home at 6:30 p.m. (I knew my friends were coming an hour later.) I had something I needed to talk with them about face-to-face. This was the first time I had made such a request.

They arrived at 6:30 sharp. Not only did they listen attentively and compassionately and respond with great encouragement, but Ray also offered help that only he could give. Over the next few days, he talked with several trusted friends who were medical experts and heads of medical institutions. The result of his networking gave me confidence that I was consulting the right doctors to learn about my different treatment options.

But most special to me was the night after surgery when he came by himself to the hospital and held my hand, simply comforting me with his presence. During this time of uncertainty, Ray represented the verse that says, "A brother is born for adversity" (Prov. 17:17 ESV).

June and Ray

𝔅⌒5⌒𝔈

GIVE TIME-TESTED ADVICE

There is no substitute for advice from someone who has been there through a similar trial, faced what you are facing. Sue, my "voice of experience" friend, gave me practical, sound advice. Some advice I really didn't want to hear, advice like, "There will be times when your body will simply stop. June, you can't just push through like you've been accustomed to doing. You'll have to allow yourself to lie down and rest." In a matter of weeks, I received a wealth of helpful, time-tested advice from around the country from others who had been there, too.

In truth, I didn't really believe that Sue's advice would apply to me until after my first chemo treatment when my body seemed to stop. My "get up and go" had "got up and went!" Perhaps that's why the Twenty-third Psalm says, "He makes me lie down in green pastures" (v. 2). Obviously this is a time when the physical body needs more rest than usual.

"Listen now to me and I will give you some advice, and may God be with you."
EXODUS 18:19

There is no substitute for advice from someone who has been there.
JUNE

June with Sue Farrar

OFFER HANDS-ON HELP

After learning about my diagnosis, Sue's daughter, who is a nurse, walked into my bedroom with tears flowing down her cheeks. Suzanne understood. She had been walking down this difficult road with her mother. She assured me that after surgery she would change my dressing and strip the tubes so I wouldn't have to make extra trips to the doctor. Immediately I thought, *Tubes? What tubes? I'll have tubes?*

Obviously, stripping the tubes was a need I had not been told about. Although I learned to drain the tubes myself, just knowing I could call on Suzanne for hands-on help was a genuine comfort. It's interesting how the Lord brought just the right people my way who had just the right abilities that I needed at the time, such as John, who carried items I couldn't lift, and Eula, who washed my hair when I couldn't raise my arms. In a very real way, they followed the example of how "the disciples, each according to his ability, decided to provide help" (Acts 11:29).

> *It's interesting how the Lord brought just the right people my way who had just the right abilities.*
> JUNE

June and Mom

PEN A MEANINGFUL POEM

Within two days of the news, I had to leave for Baltimore and New York City where I had speaking engagements. When I arrived at my hotel in Baltimore, there were flowers awaiting me from "The Mice." (Believe it or not, I belong to a small group called "The Mouseketeers." We're a group of six friends who, for over twenty years, meet together about four times a year just to support one another.) Attached was a poem penned by Randy, one of our Mouseketeers.

> To navigate some tough terrain,
> You need some friends, come shine or rain.
> You need a God to see you through,
> The Comforter who makes things new.
> You need a model of peace and duty—
> The memory of your Mother's beauty.
> You need a family that knows what it takes
> To go through trials for each others' sakes.
> You've got the best in order to ace
> This walk of faith with dignity and grace.
>
> LOVE, THE MICE[7]

After reading these words of encouragement, I immediately tucked the poem into my Bible, where it has stayed ever since. This poem was a tender connection to friends back home, reminding me of their love and support. How true, especially in times of trial, that "pleasant words are a honeycomb, sweet to the soul and healing to the bones" (Prov. 16:24).

The Mice

PLAN TO BE PRESENT

When I arrived in New York City, Kimberly, my twenty-seven-year-old niece, called from Seattle, saying, "I'm coming to Dallas!" I told her I didn't even know when the surgery would be. It didn't matter. She had ordered her nonrefundable ticket. "I don't know anything about cancer," she said, "but I want to do research, and I want us to learn as much as we can."

In reality, the ten days Kim spent in Dallas proved to be a help and a comfort beyond compare. She drove me to see my doctor, fetched food for me, and encouraged me to exercise by getting down on the floor with me! (Truthfully, I wouldn't have done those stretching exercises without her!) I think an adaptation of 2 Corinthians 7:6 says it best: "God, who comforts the downcast, comforted [me] by the coming of [Kimberly]." At another time, my sister Swanee came in from Boston to help me in a major way, and then later my sister Helen flew in from New Jersey to offer her assistance.

"I tell you the truth,
whatever you did for one of the least of these brothers of mine,
you did for me."
MATTHEW 25:40

June and niece Kim

GIVE THE GIFT OF SONG

After I returned to Dallas, I was scheduled to have a CAT scan to determine if there were any other abnormalities. My close friend Eleanor insisted not only on taking me, but also on being in the procedure room with me. While lying on the table, completely still for twenty minutes, ever so quietly—like a gentle rain—I began to hear her soft voice singing, "No One Ever Cared for Me Like Jesus."

My heart was deeply touched. So unexpected and so sweet were her spiritual songs that seldom-shed tears flowed down my cheeks. Music can touch the soul like nothing else can. I believe that's why the Bible says, "Speak to one another with psalms, hymns and spiritual songs. Sing and make music in your heart to the Lord" (Eph. 5:19). That day, Eleanor's gift of singing touched my heart as nothing else could.

A few days later I was so surprised to see another Mouseketeer friend, Rita, walk in to deliver the fruit of her own research on cancer done on my behalf. After sharing her insights, Rita picked up my guitar and sang to me from her heart, playing the most gorgeous music. Rita's rich chords and artistry have always melted my heart. That remarkable evening, Rita blessed my mind and blessed my soul. What an unexpected delight!

"Sing and make music in your heart to the Lord."
EPHESIANS 5:19

Rita and her guitar

KEEP A RECORD OF REMEMBRANCES

At the hospital, dear Eleanor had the wonderful idea of writing down all the encouraging and helpful kindnesses people extended toward me. She bought an attractive, spiral, hardback book with blank, lined pages. Using multicolored tabs, she divided the book into sections: calls, cards, flowers, food, gifts, and visits. Then within the appropriate section she recorded the name of each person who reached out to me and added a brief description of what was said or done.

When I came home from the hospital, she left the book with me so that others could continue recording each thoughtful deed. Kimberly also started a book of pictures, along with her fun, handwritten descriptions of events related to my cancer. She always seemed to have a camera in hand—even at the hospital—to capture meaningful images of loved ones visiting or attending to my needs.

Later, as I looked back on the entries in these books, I was able to write appropriate thank-you notes, but even more, the books help me remember each thoughtful deed today. What a treasure those books are to me! I can honestly say . . .

"I thank my God every time I remember you."
PHILIPPIANS 1:3

My Band-Aid Bear from Eleanor

OFFER TO COMMUNICATE PROGRESS AND NEEDS

Many people really do care. They really do want to pray. They really do want updates! The problem I seemed to have was the awkwardness of repeatedly talking about myself and volunteering information when I was not directly asked. What a relief when Kay assumed that role so thoroughly without even being asked.

As Kay gave periodic e-mail updates through "June's Journey," she kept my family and friends informed as to my progress throughout my surgery and subsequent chemotherapy and radiation treatments. It was impossible for me to keep everyone posted, and candidly, it was difficult for me to give an objective evaluation of my physical needs and legitimate concerns.

Certain people specifically asked to be included on the relatively small list. How blessed I was to have Kay take the lead and send regular e-mails stating my physical status and mentioning specific prayer requests as well as practical needs. Today, many people use websites and blogs to update friends and family with progress reports and prayer requests. The Bible says, "We have different gifts. . . . If it is serving, let him serve . . . if it is encouraging, let him encourage; if it is contributing to the needs of others, let him give generously . . . if it is showing mercy, let him do it cheerfully" (Rom. 12:6–8). At times I began to feel that Kay had all the gifts covered herself!

Left to Right: Kay, Judy, June, Eula, Connie, Jeanne

33

☙ 12 ❧

ATTEND DOCTOR APPOINTMENTS

Four friends accompanied me to multiple doctors' appointments in search of the best oncologist for me (an oncologist is a tumor specialist). They wanted not only to lend support but also to hear for themselves in order to fully understand both my illness and my treatment options. Their presence told me, *We're in this with you, no matter what!* They took notes, asked questions, processed information, and prayed fervently. (They were careful not to try to make decisions for me.)

While sharing their own perspectives, these friends stood back and allowed God to speak to me about what I should do. I was in the process of making life-altering decisions with long-term ramifications; therefore, I felt I needed guidance to make wise decisions. My four Mouseketeers applied the biblical imperative, "Let the wise listen and add to their learning, and let the discerning get guidance" (Prov. 1:5).

After interviewing four highly qualified oncologists, we all felt unanimously guided by the Lord as to which one was right for me. The five of us were in total agreement as to what God had affirmed privately in our individual hearts. What assurance that God had spoken and we all had heard Him!

Their presence told me,
"We're in this with you, no matter what!"

JUNE

13

BRING A TEDDY BEAR

The evening before surgery my doorbell rang. On my front porch was a sight I'll never forget. Five huge overstuffed bears on the shoulders of Bruce and Renee's three daughters and their two young friends—just to make sure I got a big bear hug! (Brad was the ringleader of this surprise attack.)

After seeing my sense of awe, the girls brought the bears inside my home and strategically placed the pack of bears in chairs around my dining room table. Then they placed different items in front of each bear—newspaper, Bible, concordance, and such. What a sight! (Today my studious bears still have a place of prominence around my dining table.)

Have you ever wondered, *Why are teddy bears so universally considered comforting?* I think it's because their arms are always so wide open, a position that makes us feel loved and accepted. Perhaps that was why it felt so special to receive baby bears from Janice in Las Vegas, Jim in Denver, JoAnn in Dallas, and a purple cub from Phil and Karol all the way from Kentucky.

I am well aware that Psalm 37:21 says, "the righteous give generously," but I had no idea this would include such a generous supply of teddy bears!

LIFT THE SPIRIT WITH LAUGHTER

As I was headed into surgery, friends came to the hospital with a unique sense of humor. Cheryl presented me with a pink bedpan with a potted plant placed inside. My "potty plant" evoked instant laughter from the throng of those in the waiting room! Meanwhile, Karen sent "dancing flowers" that twirled to the tune of "Cotton-Eyed Joe."

Over time, I received a bundle of humorous cards—funny cards in which I was being compared to a long-haired dog having a "bad hair day." I smiled at the note to me that said, "Don't worry about having a bad hair day—soon you won't have any hair!"

Because these cards were such fun to receive, they inspired me to write my own verses to send to others.

> If you are in pain over losing your mane,
> Just think of the lion: "bad hair days" leave him sigh'n.
> When you feel real sore 'cause your hair is no more,
> Better to have a bald head than a head full of lead.

It's interesting how a surgery that seems so serious can evoke both tears and laughter—and we all need laughter. As the Bible says, there is "a time to weep and a time to laugh" (Eccles. 3:4).

*Imagine a room full of surgery patients, literally laughing out loud,
seeing flowers twirling to "Cotton-Eyed Joe"!*
JUNE

Potty plant

PIN UP HUMOROUS POSTERS

My dear friend Diane made two hilarious posters—one for each surgery. Imagine a poster with four different candy bar wrappers glued to it: Crunch, Snickers, Butterfinger, and Air Heads. On the posters, she had glued each candy bar wrapper in place of the actual word used to spell out the message: "In a Crunch? No Snickers please. Call Dr. Butterfinger, M.D. at the Air Heads Clinic: call 1-800-BAD-GOOF!"

Her second poster—blue in color—had forty white cotton balls in the shape of a big, broad smile. Above the cotton ball smile is this clever sentiment: "What the doctors have gotten, you will fill with cotton!"

No doubt, Diane knew the reality of Proverbs 15:13, "A happy heart makes the face cheerful," and her posters brought a lot of smiles and a lot of cheer.

Say You Can Stay at the Hospital

Be available to stay in the hospital overnight. A team of friends made arrangements as to who would stay with me at the hospital. Friends Diane and June took the first surgery; Eleanor and Cheryl took the second. They fed me ice chips, put petroleum jelly on my lips, and helped me get in and out of bed. Their offer proved to be absolutely essential because, to my surprise, I had no physical stability.

Never have I more fully appreciated the literal meaning of Ecclesiastes 4:9–10, "Two are better than one. . . . If one falls down, his friend can help him up. But pity the man who falls and has no one to help him up!" The truth is that if my friends had not been there for me, I literally would have fallen! I needed to lean on my friends.

Friends Diane and June with "June the Prune"

LOOK FOR LITTLE TOKENS OF LOVE

Eleanor gave me my first token of love—a blue and white porcelain cross with these words: "Is anything too hard for GOD?" (Gen. 18:14 MESSAGE). Cheryl handed me a Noah's ark magnet to remind me that God will keep His covenant with me, and from Karen, a crocheted angel—a reminder that my guardian angel is watching over me.

Marcia gave me a little green velvet pillow with embroidered roses that simply reads, "Hugs." I love this petite pillow with its one-word message. Hugs promote emotional healing and can be freely given and received by one and all. How true that "a word aptly spoken is like apples of gold in settings of silver" (Prov. 25:11).

More creative gifts included a hand-decorated water bottle that soothed more than my aches—it warmed my heart. Cancer can be a bitter pill, but a larger-than-life capsule (filled with one hundred real pills) was a fun way to take pain relievers. It made me feel like a little kid again!

Hot water bottle and giant capsule

MAKE THE FIRST MOVE AND
SPEAK WISELY

I remember missing Maureen at our HOPE FOR THE HEART staff retreat the day after I returned from New York City (a week after confirmation of my diagnosis). I wondered why she wasn't there since she had always faithfully attended in the past. I later learned that she felt too awkward because she didn't know what to say. While she felt guilty for staying away, she also felt uneasy coming close. So I made the first move toward her.

Pam also avoided me, not because she was at a loss for words, but because my illness reminded her of her mother's recent death from cancer. Seeing me became a trigger of painful memories rising in her heart and mind, so she sought personal protection by keeping her distance. Again, I made the first move toward her, and gave her a mug with a meaningful message: "Embrace the beauty of silent moments and simple things." And I know she was glad.

Therefore, don't avoid those with cancer. And tell your loved ones, "Don't take it personally if someone fails to respond, viewing it as rejection of you, but rather view it as a reaction to cancer. Some people worry that they might upset you by saying the wrong thing. You can help them by talking openly with them. This can help alleviate their worry and fear."

When you first hear the news that someone has cancer, even if you feel at a loss for words, don't hesitate to call to say, "I'm so sorry. I care. I'm here for you and I'm praying for God's wisdom, healing, and peace for you."

Some people withdraw from their loved ones who have cancer because they don't know what to say or because it stirs up painful memories or because it's too painful to face. Instead, simply say, "I'm so sorry; I really don't know what to say." These words are sufficient—the conversation will naturally proceed from there. Meanwhile, you've let your loved one know you care.

If someone you know has cancer, don't tell bad experiences about a hospital stay or negative stories about a treatment. Instead of speaking words of horror, speak words of hope: "I know God will give you strength for whatever you need to endure. I'm praying for God's peace to be present within you, every single day."

"Be very careful, then, how you live—not as unwise but as wise,
making the most of every opportunity."
EPHESIANS 5:15–16

Share a cup of comfort.
Embrace the beauty of silent moments and simple things.

OFFER TO BE A "GOFER"

Sometimes the offer to run an errand was a lifesaver—especially when it had to do with picking up medications for pain and nausea on the way home from the hospital after surgery or prescriptions to fight nausea. (Thank you, Barbara!)

Little did I know that because of having chemo, queasiness would be a constant companion. Nor did I know that the salt in chicken soup would quell the queasiness. That's why, when I needed to be present for our ministry's International Task Force meetings, Mickey's offer to "go-fer" anything was such a big help. In a jiffy, he brought me eight cans of beef bouillon and chicken broth!

And never will I forget the Saturday afternoon when Gail emphatically informed me, "For mouth sores, take four tablets of acidophilus with goat's milk several times a day." Before I knew it, Kay was out the door and back. Did the capsules work? You bet they did; they helped within eight hours! But most memorable to me was that I didn't ever have to ask Kay for help. She simply saw a need and met it. How true that "a friend loves at all times" (Prov. 17:17) and offers to "go-fer" anything!

Prepare a Rotation Plan for Primary Home Care

Friends banded together to anticipate my future needs and to coordinate a schedule so that I wouldn't even have to *think* about the details. (For several weeks, three friends—Eleanor, June, and Barbara—rotated each night, sleeping on a flip bed in my bedroom.) They set in motion a plan for accomplishing each task so that I did not even have to ask for help.

It was beautiful to see them working together to provide for my needs, not with the intent of doing what they would most enjoy doing, but rather doing what I really needed. Even though I knew the situation was burdensome, they didn't make me feel as though I was a burden. With sweet attentiveness and joyful spirits they carried out Paul's directive to "carry each other's burdens, and in this way you will fulfill the law of Christ" (Gal. 6:2).

It was beautiful to see them working together
to provide for my needs.
JUNE

Eleanor, Barbara, and June

ಲ21ಲ

Bring Helpful Books, Videos, and Booklets

Val and Susan sent three books on cancer that they knew would be helpful, and Suzanne gave me two others. Nancy sent me a video. People from all over the country—people who I didn't know personally—were amazingly caring in that regard. They and other friends gave me pamphlets, articles, and advice about people who had already walked this challenging path.

I was eager to receive authoritative information, for the more I learned, the more confident I felt. I was eager to "listen to advice and accept instruction" because I knew Proverbs 19:20 said, "in the end you will be wise."

Initially, I knew very little about cancer. Although my father had died of colon cancer and my mother of liver cancer, I barely knew the basics. I needed to know more. For example:

- What is cancer? Cancer or *carcinoma* is a malignant, uncontrolled growth of cells.[8]
- When does cancer begin? Cancer begins when a normal cell changes into a cell with an abnormal growth pattern—a cell that abnormally divides and grows.
- How fast does breast cancer grow? An average tumor doubles every one hundred days. When it reaches one centimeter (3/8 inch)—the size of the tip of your smallest finger—it has been in your body approximately eight to ten years. This tumor has grown from one cell to approximately 100 billion cells.[9]
- How does cancer spread (or metastasize)? When cancer cells break away from their original location, they can travel through the blood vessels or lymph system to other sites and form secondary tumors. This spreading to a distant site is called metastasis.

My number-one objective regarding cancer has been to do all that I can to eradicate any microscopic cells that may have metastasized in my body. (Chemotherapy and antiestrogen therapy kill metastatic cells.)

Friends gave me pamphlets, articles, and advice about people who had already walked this challenging path.

JUNE

44

ASK APPROPRIATE QUESTIONS

From the moment I received my diagnosis, and throughout the next nine months, I felt as if I had been swept away by a mammoth tidal wave and swiftly carried off to some unfamiliar country where everyone spoke a strange language—at least a language totally foreign to my ears. Clearly, I did not know the lingo of cancer.

Consequently, my crash course in "Cancer 101" proved to be invaluable—but only so because of my loved ones who also entered into the "schooling" by listening and asking appropriate questions. Getting as much information as possible concerning my particular types of cancer (I had two types) was essential. Educating ourselves is particularly helpful because knowledge instills confidence and a degree of control over our lives. Knowledge also decreases fear and anxiety. Therefore, following surgery and prior to the meeting with my oncologist, we tried to compile a list of questions, such as:

- What is the size of the tumor(s)? I had two tumors, both classified as T2.

Tumor Classifications[10] *(measured in centimeters)*

T0	No tumor is reported and there are no signs of spreading to lymph nodes or tissues beyond the breast.
T1	2 centimeters (cm) or smaller
T2	2–5 cm
T3	5+ cm
T4	Any size tumor that has spread to the chest wall or skin.

- What is the stage of the cancer? Breast cancer is identified by stages. Mine was Stage II because it was under 5 cm, it wasn't in the lymph nodes, and it had not metastasized.

Cancer Stages[11]

Stage I	T1 with no lymph nodes involved or with cancer in a lymph node under 2 millimeters (mm) in size

Stage II   T0–T2 with lymph node involvement over 2 mm in size
             T2–T3 with zero lymph nodes involved
Stage III   T0–T3 with bulky lymph node involvement
             T3 or 4 with lymph node involvement
Stage IV   Any size tumor that has metastasized (spread to a distant
             location)

- Does the cancer have other important tumor characteristics? My lymph nodes were clear.
- What are the options for treatment? Surgery, chemotherapy, radiation, hormone blockers—I had it all!
- What are the percentages of benefit (cure rates) for each option?
- What are the risks of each option? What are the possible temporary and long-term side effects, and how should they be treated?

See "Tips for Temporary Trials" on page 87.

- Is the cancer estrogen-receptor positive? Mine was. Therefore, I was told that taking a hormone blocker could be highly effective to avoid the recurrence of cancer.
- Is the tumor slowgrowing or fastgrowing? I had one of each—lucky me!
- What is the likelihood of recurrence after treatment? What year markers are significant to pass? For example, once I passed 3½ years with no recurrence of cancer, I rejoiced because fast-growing cancer typically recurs within the first 2 to 3 years.
- Is this type of cancer genetic? BRCA-1 and/or BRCA-2 genetic testing can determine whether there is a susceptibility to hereditary cancer genes. Ninety-five percent of breast cancer is not hereditary, and my cancer was not.[12]
- Are there known causes for this kind of cancer? Mine was unknown.
- What helpful books, materials, or support groups would you recommend?

Realize that no question is stupid or unimportant—especially when it concerns the physical, mental, or emotional health of anyone going through cancer treatment. We all need to ask as many questions as necessary in order to make informed decisions and to feel a sense of responsibility for our treatment. That is why the Bible says that "the heart of the discerning acquires knowledge; the ears of the wise seek it out" (Prov. 18:15).

23

INVEST ENERGY IN THE
INTERNET

You can search the Internet for extensive information on any illness or on any cancer. Imagine my surprise when one evening Rita walked into my home with reams of paper—three days' worth of research on cancer! I could hardly believe the time and energy she invested. She lived out Proverbs 15:14, "The discerning heart seeks knowledge."

One fact is clear—after you read page after page after page on the Internet, you are able to distill the major points into simple, understandable terms. For example, it really helps to understand how different treatments for cancer work.

How Does Chemotherapy Work?[13]

- Chemotherapy is the use of toxic drugs in an attempt to destroy cancer cells. While surgery and radiation remove and destroy cancer cells in a specific area, chemotherapy works to kill cancer throughout the entire body.
- Chemo also affects normal, healthy cells, causing side effects that typically impact the blood, hair, mouth, digestive tract, and reproductive system. Some people feel minimal impact, while others experience greater effects.
- More than one hundred chemotherapy drugs are used in various combinations (combination chemotherapy). Each drug performs a different function and works together to kill more cancer cells.

How Does Radiation Work?[14]

- Radiation therapy beams specific doses of high-energy waves (X-rays) at tumors or areas of the body where tumors have been removed or where there is disease.
- These high doses of radiation kill cancerous cells or keep them from growing and reproducing (dividing into two cells).

How Does Hormone Therapy Work?[15]

- Some cancer growths are fed by the hormones estrogen and progesterone.
- Oral drugs called hormone blockers are needed to either lower or block the hormone levels in order to prevent the recurrence of cancer.

---

*It really helps to understand
how different treatments for cancer work.*

JUNE

Exert Initiative to Exercise

A few days following each surgery, I needed to begin a regime of regular exercise—I needed to stretch muscles that were naturally drawing up during the healing process. But exercise was an unwanted companion because it was too uncomfortable.

To encourage me to do what I didn't want to do, Kim came in with a cheery voice: "Let's do some exercise!" Well, I didn't want to disappoint my niece and seem like a fuddy-duddy, so I would do whatever she wanted me to do. What a help!

Starting a new habit is not easy and requires setting aside needed time in your daily schedule. It takes dedication to the cause and determination to reach the goal. Encourage your loved one who is facing this physical and mental challenge, offer to make exercise a twosome for the first week or so, and lead the two of you in the required exercises. Just having someone there to share the experience, to acknowledge the difficulty, and to cheer the accomplishments will give incentive and prevent procrastination.

If your loved one feels physically discouraged, you might share these words of wisdom: "I can do everything through him who gives me strength" (Phil. 4:13).

25

Buy New Sleepwear

Surgery makes mobility difficult at best. That's why the two identical gifts—intentionally identical gowns (one from Lillian, the other from her daughter, Barbara)—were such a relief. They knew I would adore the soft, new, blue plaid gowns.

The fact that they buttoned down the front made them easier and less painful to get on and off (my arms didn't want to cooperate). Barbara and Lillian knew the gown ordeal would be a challenge after surgery. Adding to their thoughtfulness, they also gave me a blue plaid robe to match!

My friend June also gave me a soft, blue cotton gown for the hotter months—again, one that buttoned down the front. (I had no idea that my skin would be so sensitive following surgery.)

The Bible says, "God loves a cheerful giver" (2 Cor. 9:7). God sure must love my friends!

New nightgown

Offer Help for the Holidays

Three years before my cancer "ambush," my dear friend Sue was facing her own battle with the disease. I asked Sue if I could help with her Christmas shopping—she was just too weak to shop. Not surprisingly, she had clear ideas of the gifts she wanted to give each person on her list—specifically her three children, their spouses, and her three grandchildren.

Going by name, Sue and I made a detailed list of two gifts per person—eighteen in all—then I hit the stores. By Christmas, Sue's close family members all had gifts under their trees from their fun-filled Nanna, just as they had in the past.

This idea could easily be adapted for those who wish to send Christmas cards but don't have the strength. First, bring several card options from which to choose. Once a favorite card is selected, you can address and stamp the envelopes (attractive Christmas-themed stamps abound during the holidays), have your loved one sign each card, then you stuff, seal, and mail them. Consider recruiting friends to divide up the task and share in the blessing.

Comfy chair from Swanee

Before my second surgery, my Boston sister, Swanee, announced that she was flying to Dallas to take care of me throughout the Thanksgiving holidays. "Your friends can all be with their families, and that will give them some needed time off." Instead of traditionally being with her husband's family, Swanee flew in Wednesday evening and stayed until Sunday evening.

Since my mobility was sorely lacking following two surgeries, she was extremely helpful—beyond description. She even bought me a leather rocker recliner, which made getting up much easier with an "alley-oop." Swanee exemplified Joshua 1:14–15: "You are to help your brothers [and sister!] until the LORD gives them rest. . . ." Oh, did she help!

51

Fix Enough Food ... for Caregivers, Too

No "sick bay" list could be complete without the mention of "meals on wheels." From Linda to Lillian, Kathy to Kelli, Muriel to Maggie, Jane, Jack, and Janie, every morsel brought over by friends satisfied palates and helped to lighten the load of my caregivers.

On Thanksgiving Day, Kelli took to heart Nehemiah 8:10, "Go and enjoy choice food and sweet drinks, and send some to those who have nothing prepared." She sent over a scrumptious, multicourse dinner for my sister and me. Lillian provided our dining entertainment by quoting a precious Christmas poem she had memorized as a child.

One day my nephew Hunter and his new wife, Stephanie, came to see me. I was still bedridden. They made me feel like a queen holding court—bedside. They brought some delectable food, but most of all, I valued their making time to visit. Then, a few weeks later, Ashlee, Hunter's sister, dropped by with a mouthwatering Italian dish that was immensely appreciated by everyone. Within the month, my niece was back again with her "meals on wheels."

Those who came with food were extra caring—bringing food in disposable containers that didn't need to be returned. That's extra thoughtful!

*Every morsel brought over by friends satisfied palates and helped
to lighten the load of my caregivers.*

JUNE

What a surprise! The day before Christmas my nineteen-year-old nephew Tanner arrived at my home and presented me with an "Aunt" mug with a crazy hairdo. Inside the mug is the sentiment, "The bonds we have are everlasting." What a meaningful moment!

Bring a Bouquet, Plant, or Helium Balloon

There's a reason why flowers are typically sent during times of sadness or sickness. Flowers bring beauty to people in pain—floral bouquets bring "sunshine" to any setting.

On the other hand, a plant can last for months and sometimes for years. For example, following my first surgery, Bob and Ruth brought to my bedside a small but sturdy green plant in a classic, blue and white porcelain container, and it's still hearty and thriving, providing constant comfort.

But check first—because I was surprised to learn shortly before this book was published that flowers and plants may present a cause for concern. My cousin, Brent, shared the following information when his sweet wife, Elaine, began her first course of chemotherapy:

- No cut flowers or plants. We are removing all indoor plants and flowers as they tend to shed mold into the air and can be a source of infection. Cut flowers are also a risk item as, for example, the water in the vase of flowers often harbors infectious bacteria, mold, and mildew, which can evaporate into the air and spread to the patient.
- No gardening. We have just learned that chemotherapy patients should not be in contact with soil as it is a huge source of bacteria and mold, which presents an unnecessary danger.[16]

Of course, a huge helium balloon with bright ribbons and bows and a big smiley face was a tremendous hit. Such a gift would brighten any corner! Understandably, the clever "cookie bouquet" was irresistible—especially to those with a sweet tooth.

The good news is, whether it's a bouquet from Gil and Ann, a plant, or a balloon from Ray and Nancy Ann, they each say, "We care. You matter. You are loved."

"Like cold water to a weary soul is good news from a distant land."
PROVERBS 25:25

Seek Ways to Assuage Anxiety

The day of my first chemotherapy treatment, Barbara arrived early at my home simply to pray with me. What a time for prayer—I needed peace. Then, after my friend June drove me to the hospital, she sought to calm my apprehension by reading the December 7 selections from both of the classic daily devotionals, *Streams in the Desert* and *My Utmost for His Highest*.

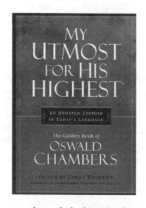

Classic daily devotional

I'll have to admit that I had difficulty concentrating because of all the "horror stories" I had heard about chemotherapy. But I so appreciated her efforts and valued her concern. And reading to me did calm some of my anxiety.

Then, "out of the blue," as I was walking into the treatment center, my sister Swanee called from Boston just to give me a boost. What a surprise! Her call was the encouragement that I sorely needed.

Apparently, they all had discerned that I might feel anxious prior to my first chemo series—and they were right. They gave me just what I needed that unforgettable day. They did what the Scripture says to do . . .

"Encourage one another and build each other up."
1 THESSALONIANS 5:11

ᏠᏎ30ᏜᏋ

HELP TO HUNT FOR HEAD COVERS

Set to undergo aggressive chemo, I knew I would lose my hair between days fourteen and eighteen following my first treatment. So wig shopping quickly surfaced at the top of my to-do list. But I had one minor problem: wigs were a totally unfamiliar territory!

Fortunately, my sister-in-law Nancy Ann researched the wig shops in Dallas. And on day fourteen, my friend June took me to a wig store suggested by both Nancy Ann and Maggie. Although truly grateful for their input, I still remember sitting in the car outside the store—with tears in my eyes—thinking, *I can't believe this is happening—this is so surreal!*

Yet my cancer was very real. So I took a deep breath, slowly stepped out of my car, and made the decision to face this new unwanted experience with faith, not with fear. This was a faith that I would trust the Lord with every step of this "fascinating" journey as long as I had breath.

Truthfully, I just never expected to have to take "Wig Education 101." But I'll admit that I learned more about wigs than I ever thought possible—and I'm still learning. For example:

- Wearing a wig cap underneath keeps a wig from slipping.
- Wigs can be taped on or glued on and can stay on for weeks.
- As new hair grows back, a weave or clip-on hair extensions can add instant length.
- When you find a wig you really like, buy two if possible. Wig styles are often discontinued, and wigs wear out.
- Quality human-hair wigs are typically more expensive than synthetic ones. Many novice wig shoppers expect their human-hair wigs to be fuss free. Well, they aren't. They still need styling just like natural hair. Unlike synthetics, these wigs can be dyed, highlighted, and curled with heat appliances.
- Synthetic wigs hold their style well. However, synthetics typically don't last as long, and some can look unnaturally shiny. Likewise, synthetic hair cannot tolerate heat or chemical dyes.

Actually, wigs have come a long way. Both human hair and synthetics are available in an unlimited number of colors, styles, and textures, and are also adjustable with elastic bands inside. In truth, they are much easier to care for than your own natural hair. And today, synthetic wigs can look exactly like your real human hair. With the right match, no one will even know you are wearing a wig. But realize this—it's always good to take a friend with you to help choose what looks good on you.

Wig prices vary depending on where you shop. You can find reasonably priced human hair wigs if you do your homework. Synthetic wigs should not be underestimated because they look great and are less costly to replace. My friend Maggie—known for her humor—said, "If someone asks, 'Is that your hair?' say, 'It sure is—I paid a pretty penny for it!'" After trying on a synthetic wig, I realized, "I like this wig better than my own hair—this isn't so bad after all!"

And sweet Nicole sent me a care package of wonderful stretch head coverings in a variety of colors. They were intended to warm my bald head so I would not catch "a death of a cold" (as my grandmother used to say).

I mused, since the Bible says that "even the very hairs of your head are all numbered," if I'm wearing a wig, will He still keep count of every strand of hair?[17]

June willingly "bared" her bare head. Pictured here
in her "mangy moose" sweatshirt as adopted mom,
Lillian Spruill, encourages with a heartfelt hug.

June and Swanee with hats

Soon after getting my first wig, my brother-in-law Charles empathetically donned a "Goofy" hat for an entire evening so I wouldn't feel as uncomfortable wearing my own unfamiliar head covering.

June with a wig

༄31ca

ENCOURAGE A
"JOURNAL FOR THE JOURNEY"

Journaling can take many forms. Some people feel emotionally stuck in their pain. Journaling can help them get unstuck!

When people process their experiences on paper, the act of writing down thoughts and feelings—expressing anxieties and fears—can be an immensely healing process. Some emotions are difficult to express. Keeping a journal of the daily struggles and victories, along with the thoughts that accompany them, can be a cathartic exercise. Blank pages at the back of this book can be used to jot down notes and thoughts!

Encourage your loved one to consider journaling in order to help draw out difficult emotions that need to be surfaced. Later, he or she can look back at the journal and help someone else on the same journey. "The purposes of a man's heart are deep waters, but a man of understanding draws them out" (Prov. 20:5).

What you are reading right now is a type of journal about my own journey through cancer. Writing down all the different ways that people reached out and blessed me has, in turn, enabled me to reach out and bless others.

The act of writing thoughts and feelings can be an
immensely healing process.
JUNE

MAKE A CHART FOR MEDICATIONS

Connie, a faithful assistant, contributed a valuable treasure. She constructed a chart of the various medications I was to take. It contained the name of each pill, each injection, and each fluid with a description of its purpose and the time each was to be taken throughout my treatment regimen. This wonderfully detailed chart grew over time and proved to be invaluable both to me and to my caregivers.

With pills and shots being added along the way, by the time I'd had my fourth chemotherapy treatment, I couldn't go even a few hours without taking a pill, giving myself an injection, eating a particular food, or drinking a particular drink. Keeping the schedule straight seemed next to impossible.

Connie's chart saved me from feeling that I was drowning in a sea of medications. I needed help in holding on to my doctor's instructions in order to do what was truly best for my physical body! "Hold on to instruction, do not let it go; guard it well, for it is your life" (Prov. 4:13).

Medicine Chart

Medicine	Purpose	Dosage	Time
A	Nausea	1 Pill	8, 12, 4
B	Blood Count	10 mg Shot	12
C	Pain	1 Patch	Every 48 hrs.
D	Fatigue	8 oz.	10, 6
E	Iron	1 Pill	8

Remind Gently of the Routine

"Have you taken all of your pills yet? Do you need your antinausea meds? What about your antibiotics?"

Is asking such questions necessary? Normally, I wouldn't think so; however, after my fourth cycle of chemotherapy, I think I slipped into "chemo brain." Yes, you read it correctly: CHEMO BRAIN! (When I first heard about chemo brain, I laughed out loud!) Apparently, after a certain number of treatments, the memory can be temporarily affected.

I've even read that chemo brain (or chemo fog) can last up to ten years! As a result, I've told everyone I know that I'm going to take full advantage of this label for as long as I can. Anytime I forget anything, I get to claim chemo brain. In fact, I told all of my friends that I would share the label with them so that when they are forgetful, they too can claim chemo brain by osmosis. (They love it.)

In truth, gentle reminders were welcomed friends to me— "friends"—because of the times I tended to forget something important. I am grateful to my faithful family of friends who have enabled me to be wiser because of their helpful hints. They were most aware that "wisdom preserves the life of its possessor" (Eccles. 7:12).

For times when June had "chemo brain,"
this little porcelain plaque said it all!

FIND ITEMS FREQUENTLY FORGOTTEN

Karen, whom I've never met, sent a small basket—the perfect size to hold my pill bottles. This was a basket she had ordered for herself, but instead sent it to me. How helpful and how selfless! Don, a longtime friend, brought his favorite CD of songs that he has loved for years. Pat knew of my tendency to be very cold natured and brought soft, warm blankets to ward off the cold.

And my dear friend Dorothy, the queen of hospitality and practicality, didn't limit her generosity to just one item, but instead sent an assortment of little treasures:

- thank-you cards and stamps
- a bag of hard candy for the "nurses"
- a pocket-sized case with three pill bottles
- two crossword puzzle books with pencils
- a card of encouragement containing a message from the heart of God: "When you pass through the waters, I will be with you; and when you pass through the rivers, they will not sweep over you. When you walk through the fire, you will not be burned; the flames will not set you ablaze" (Isa. 43:2).

Thanks to Dorothy, I could express gratitude to others through the cards she so thoughtfully sent to me.

PUT TOGETHER A SCRAPBOOK
OF PICTURES

Every few days I seemed to receive a surprise treat from Helen, my New York/New Jersey sister. Initially Helen asked me if there was anything that I would like. I answered, "Yes, I would love some family pictures."

In a matter of days, the first scrapbook arrived. It was full of fun family pictures that brought back many memories. Obviously, Helen went through bundles of snapshots, cut out the important part of the selected pictures, and then contoured each photograph, giving them a special animated look. The second scrapbook was also an endearing labor of love. I will treasure these keepsakes for a lifetime!

And so special is Helen's hand-drawn Scripture, that it is now displayed on my bedroom wall: "God hath not given us the spirit of fear; but of power, and of love, and of a sound mind" (2 Tim. 1:7 KJV).

There is nothing like seeing truth every day
to keep me free from fear.
JUNE

Helen's scrapbook

Fix Food That Helps with Healing

Can you imagine not having any desire to eat steak? Well, because of chemotherapy, I experienced some surprising changes. I lost my desire for sweets (that was actually good), and I lost my desire for meats (that was not so good).

Because I had such difficulty chewing meat (due to mouth sores), and because I continually struggled with a low red blood cell count (I was anemic), Jack came to my home, donned his chef's hat, and prepared a steak. More accurately, he simmered a number of steaks for me to drink! Jack knew I needed the beneficial nutrients in red meat.

Chef Jack's Beef Broth

2 lbs. round roast or steak
1 Crock-Pot
Cut meat into small pieces and put into the Crock-Pot.
Cook on Low overnight.

Pour broth into a pint jar, and put meat in a strainer and squeeze. Press with a spoon until all the broth is removed. Refrigerate. When chilled, remove fat with a spoon. When ready to serve, pour into a cup, heat, and serve.

(Note: If your loved one's liver has difficulty processing iron, check with your doctor before preparing this high-protein broth.)

Bon appétit from Chef Jack![18]

> *"[The Lord] satisfies your desires with good things so that your youth is renewed like the eagle's."*
> PSALM 103:5

Jack and his pot

Help Your Loved One Live
with Lymphedema

In February I flew to Nashville to speak at a large convention. That evening I was shocked to see that my right hand and arm were red and swollen—they seemed huge! Immediately I called my oncologist, who told me to come see her as soon as I returned. She explained that the swelling in my arm was lymphedema, an accumulation of lymphatic fluid in soft tissues, which causes swelling ("edema" refers to swelling).

Between 20 and 30 percent of those who have had lymph nodes removed experience lymphedema.[19] If your loved one is experiencing this sort of swelling, encourage him or her to seek a doctor's help.

Our blood carries lymphatic fluid, which contains many good nutrients, throughout our bodies. Lymph nodes filter out bacteria, toxins, and waste products from the lymphatic fluid. Think of lymphedema as a plumbing problem. Our veins and lymphatic channels are like pipes and drains meant to handle the normal flow of lymphatic fluid. If these lymph nodes and channels are removed, we may not have enough pipes and drains to eliminate all the fluid.

Upon return, I received a lymph massage, a special type of wrapping, and a pressure sleeve and gauntlet. Every time I fly in an airplane, I must wear my pressure sleeve to avoid swelling.

Wearing a pressure sleeve for the arm and a pressure gauntlet for the hand will help alleviate swelling. Meanwhile, remember that "we are hard pressed on every side, but not crushed; perplexed, but not in despair" (2 Cor. 4:8).

Pressure sleeve and gauntlet

ॐ 38 ॐ

PROVIDE COMFY CLOTHES

Forget about my former pullover sweaters—or pullover anything! I had no idea how sensitive my skin would be after surgery. That is why I was so grateful when Nancy Ann brought an assortment of comfy button-up tops (as well as desserts to die for and a stuffed cat stitched with "You're the cat's meow").

Just think, you may be the angel of mercy who God will use to provide loose-fitting clothing and shoes for your friend by either loaning them or purchasing them. (Some items on loan are appropriate because after chemotherapy much of the fluid retention and weight gain is lost.) Just make sure the clothing doesn't irritate or put pressure on the skin, especially on areas sensitive as a result of cancer treatment.

The issue of clothes began to be a problem as I looked forward to Heather's wedding. Ray and Nancy Ann's daughter was getting married, and because of the steroids in my chemo medication, I had ballooned up an extra thirty-five pounds and couldn't wear anything I owned that was appropriate for a wedding.

How well I remember the day when Nancy Ann called me at HOPE FOR THE HEART. She knew I was not able to endure the rigors of shopping, so she brought the shop to me! She was on her way with five outfits that she had handpicked for me to try on. One was simply perfect!

Since the Bible says that "it is more blessed to give than to receive" (Acts 20:35), Nancy Ann surely must be blessed!

Ray and Nancy Ann

BE SENSITIVE ABOUT
SPECIAL OCCASIONS

Four weeks before my niece Heather's wedding, I could no longer wear any of the shoes that I owned—my feet were too swollen. One day I was talking with my brother on the telephone and shared my predicament. "Ray, I've gained so much weight, and there's absolutely nothing I can do to stop it!"

Never will I forget his words: "June, it doesn't matter. We just want you there for the wedding. You can come barefoot!" Wow! He would not be embarrassed—even if I looked like a blimp. (Tears came to my eyes. He never knew.) He just wanted me there to share in the special occasion.

How good of him to speak such comforting words in the midst of my embarrassment. As Proverbs 15:23 says, "A man finds joy in giving an apt reply—and how good is a timely word!"

As I donned my new size ten shoes (normally size nine) for the wedding, I gave thanks that I wouldn't have to walk down the aisle barefoot! On the evening of the wedding reception, my sister Swanee was phenomenal. Bless her heart, she knew I needed help, and without a word from me, she took on the job. And what a help she was! She offered her hand to help me up the stairs. (I could stand without back pain for only a few minutes.)

During the reception she seated me in a chair to ease my pain, and then as she mingled among guests, she proceeded to escort friends and family over to where she had me stationed. Later, when I had to leave early (the one and only time I've ever left early from anything!), Swanee left her family at the hotel, drove me home, put me to bed, stayed the night, and helped me the next morning to get ready for the "day after" brunch. Truly, her sensitivity was endearing and her servanthood was extraordinary. Swanee indeed lived out "serve one another in love" (Gal. 5:13).

"A man finds joy in giving an apt reply."
PROVERBS 15:23

Be Ready to Donate Blood

As the chemo treatments took their toll on my body, they also assaulted my blood. Platelets play a crucial part in the blood clotting process by forming a "platelet plug," which stops bleeding and allows injuries to heal. Simply put, my platelets were dangerously low.

Because I had a low platelet count, I bruised easily. I had difficulty stopping nosebleeds as well as normal bleeding from the needle pricks. Thus, I needed several platelet transfusions—ASAP! My friend June drove me to the hospital and immediately donated blood. Within the hour, Cheryl called and volunteered to do the same. However, a chaplain who worked at the hospital had just walked in to donate blood for anyone (me, in this case) who needed it.

Though I never had the opportunity to thank that chaplain, I literally thank God for people like him who are so willing to give of themselves. (In an effort to track down the chaplain, I have since learned that many chaplains and hospital staff members donate their blood on a regular basis.)

Many people are unaware that an excessively low platelet count can cause a person literally to bleed to death internally. This health risk must be taken seriously. In fact, I was not allowed to travel more than twenty minutes from the hospital just in case bleeding started and didn't stop. The Bible has made it clear that "the life of a creature is in the blood" (Lev. 17:11). Therefore, realize that when you volunteer to give your blood, you are actually saving a life!

CONVEY GOD'S HOPE ON
HEART-SHAPED CUTOUTS

One of the most creative gifts I received was a red, heart-shaped candy box (minus the candy) filled with many personalized messages. Someone I do not know personally—a dedicated listener to our daily broadcasts from HOPE FOR THE HEART—cut out about twenty small, medium, and large paper hearts from pink construction paper. On each heart she wrote a different Scripture that included the word *heart*, and then she personalized each Scripture with my name.

How precious to see Psalm 69:32 (KJV) written at the top, followed by the words: "The humble shall see this, and be glad: and your **heart** [June] shall live."

And another, "Give . . . thy servant [June] an understanding **heart** to judge thy people, that [she] may discern between good and bad" (1 Kings 3:9 KJV).

And still another, "I have found [June] . . . a [woman] after my own **heart**" (Acts 13:22).

Oh, how these tender messages warmed my heart!

Heart message

CONSIDER A
CANCER SUPPORT GROUP

Several years before my illness, two of my neighbors were diagnosed with cancer. One day, Carolyn told me about the cancer support group that was held at her home and what a blessing it was for her, as well as for Ruth. They could laugh together, cry together, and be unguarded before each other—together. Among old and new friends they were able to talk about their frustrations and fears, how to face the future, and about how they could each help their husbands, help their children, help each other, and help even themselves.

Perhaps you could encourage your loved one to join such a group; perhaps help find a group and then go to the first meeting with your friend. Although I wasn't in that group, because of the help from my extraordinary friends, I learned the vital role of heartfelt support, care, and encouragement. I could honestly say to them, "Your love has given me great joy and encouragement" (Philem. 1:7). I couldn't have made it without them.

Plan a Regular Time to Pray

Recently, I saw Dave at a large, festive gathering, and we began to talk. At the conclusion of our conversation, his words were a surprise to me: "June, I want you to know that a day doesn't go by that I do not pray for you. I pray for you every day." I was deeply moved and amazed—I had no idea.

Just as discipline is required when establishing a new habit or beginning a new routine, discipline is also needed when planning to pray for your loved one on a regular basis. Look at your schedule and determine the time each day when you can arrange to be alone with God and lift up your loved one to Him. (I know that my cousin, Swanlou, and my mother's precious friend, Hannah, pray each day for me.)

Give your loved one an opportunity to express needs and concerns so that you can pray knowledgeably. Specifically ask, "What would you like for me to pray about?" or "What is most challenging for you right now?" And if possible, let your loved one know the exact time you will be praying.

"Far be it from me that I should sin against the LORD
by failing to pray for you."
1 SAMUEL 12:23

June and Hannah

Consider a Cancer Walk

My heart was encouraged when I realized that my loved ones were not only concerned about my individual battle with cancer, but also cared about defeating cancer for everyone else. The American Cancer Society sponsors a cancer walk designed to raise awareness, foster camaraderie, and raise funds for breast cancer research, patient services, education, and advocacy.

Participants can walk in their own cities. My sister Helen walked in my name in her local cancer walk on the East Coast, and my niece Kim participated in a minitriathlon on the West Coast. My friend Janie did a walk to raise funds in Dallas, while her husband, Jack, rode a motorcycle to provide safety for the Dallas walkers. Little did they know that Janie herself would later be diagnosed with cancer. Now in remission, Janie says

Janie at a cancer walk

she and Jack turned to the first edition of this book over and over for practical help. How special to know that their efforts could help defeat this common enemy.

Helen walked in New Jersey, not to solicit funds, but to love and support me. She wrote to our family members encouraging them to walk around the block and to think of me during that time. What a marvelous act of love from my family!

A year after my surgery it was my turn. I was blessed to be able to encourage Val by sponsoring her fundraising walk for Susan. I personally believe that a cancer walk offers encouragement to the sponsor and to the walker, as well as to the person battling cancer.

Those who support cancer patients can pray this Scripture for them: "He gives strength to the weary and increases the power of the weak. . . . Those who hope in the LORD will renew their strength. They will soar on wings like eagles; they will run and not grow weary, they will walk and not be faint" (Isa. 40:29–31).

45

GIVE AN ENGRAVED BRACELET

After my diagnosis, my "forever friend" Barbara learned that she had breast cancer. This news hit many of us hard because my joyful, easy-going friend—who is always helping others—is anything but sickly. Barbara is not just a staff counselor, but also an inspiring friend "who walks her talk!"

The team within our Christian counseling ministry wanted to do something extra special for Barbara, so we decided to give her a wide-band, slip-on, silver bracelet. On the outside is engraved, "Fear not, for I am with you" (Isa. 41:10 ESV). Engraved on the inside are the initials of each staff member—all forty-eight of us!

Today as she wraps the bracelet around her wrist, it serves as a constant reminder of our love for her and our prayers to God on her behalf. The silver band also serves as a comforting assurance from the Lord, who says, "Do not fear, for I am with you; do not be dismayed, for I am your God. I will strengthen you and help you; I will uphold you with my righteous right hand" (Isa. 41:10).

Barbara's bracelet

HELP OUT AT HOME

While some say, "A man's home is his castle," maintaining the castle can be a challenge when someone in the family is in recovery. The extraordinary thoughtfulness of my loved ones was quite evident by their willingness to keep my home in order.

Vacuuming and sweeping, laundering and lifting are easy before surgery—but right after surgery, these tasks are impossible. Offering to mow the lawn, empty the trash, and do small repairs are wonderful ways to help.

Not having to worry about housework or yard work is a great gift! Often I found it difficult to ask for personal help, yet I can unequivocally say that these words reflect the compassionate care of my sacrificial helpers: "You will do even more than I ask" (Philem. 1:21).

While my friend Barbara was recovering, one of the most practical expressions of friendship was the practical help of Jim and Phyllis, who regularly vacuumed the floor, prepared the meals, and washed the dishes. Although I was sleeping on a flip bed at the foot of Barbara's bed at night and helping with odds and ends during the day, these friends would call ahead before coming over and ask "What do you need us to bring?"

Inevitably, there were always a few small items like milk and liquid detergent. Jim and Phyllis came over almost every evening for several weeks following surgery to help do whatever needed to be done—even putting up pictures. Their presence was a true expression of Christian love.

"Love is patient, love is kind."

1 CORINTHIANS 13:4

COMMUNICATE YOUR CARE
WITH CARDS

During the first few months following my diagnosis, hardly a day went by that I did not receive a note or card of encouragement. The wonderful words and special Scriptures still bring comfort to my heart—comfort beyond imagination.

From colorful cards with stickers to decorative handwritten letters, I clearly see that creativity knows no bounds. Each letter—some from people whom I don't even know—is meaningful. Each piece of correspondence is cherished because someone took personal time to write.

Beside my bed was a big basket of notes, letters, and cards. At times when my heart would be down, these notes quickly cheered me up. Today I'm much more aware that "an anxious heart weighs [me] down, but a kind word cheers [me] up" (Prov. 12:25).

Can personal messages from people we don't know have any real ministry? Oh, yes! The following letter from twenty-year-old Teresa in Fargo, North Dakota, blessed me beyond measure:

> I think of you and how much you mean to my heart, and I imagine there must be at least 1,000,000 others that feel the same way. Especially when you start your chemo, always remember that you don't have to do this alone. There's a reason why God created others, and everybody needs an opportunity to serve someone else . . . and soon enough you may very well be the one to give others that chance.
>
> My grandma, seventy-eight, also has cancer, and it has almost completely taken over her earthly body. She's what one would call a "living saint." I visited her about a week ago, and she had come to the point where she was really down. I asked her how it felt being so close to the one goal she's had all her life: seeing Jesus face-to-face. She said, "I'm really excited, and I have a great peace." So then I said, "Then why the long face?" Her servant-of-servants heart replied that she's not doing much to serve the Lord. Physically speaking, she's unable to serve the Lord.
>
> Then I brought to her mind how she's helping others by allowing others to visit her, clothe her, feed her . . . all those super

humbling things. She's helping them to be more like Jesus . . . because that's what HE would have done. She seemed to glow in the dark after the realization of that.

Teresa's sentiments ministered to my soul! Her letter helped me change my perspective to more readily allow others to give to me without my feeling that I was imposing. I needed that change of perspective.

"Encourage one another daily."
HEBREWS 3:13

BE PREPARED TO HELP FOR THE
LONG HAUL

It is not unusual for visits, calls, and offers of help to taper off after a couple weeks. When someone calls and a cheery voice answers, the assumption can be made that all is well and help is no longer needed. However, this is sometimes far from the truth.

Even when spirits are high and recovery is going well, it doesn't mean that needs are no longer present, especially when a loved one is undergoing chemo or radiation treatments and energy is low. The side effects of these treatments can render anyone incapable of performing simple tasks that are suddenly too strenuous to accomplish.

Be committed to being available for the long haul and to continue helping throughout the length of the cancer treatments. Such perseverance and faithfulness will be forever remembered and deeply appreciated.

"[Love] . . . always hopes, always perseveres."
1 CORINTHIANS 13:7

it's hard to put
Love in a box but
you can wrap a
Person in a
hug.

Put "To-Do" Tasks on a Tray

Typically, caring friends want to "do something" and often say, "Let me know what I can do to help." At that moment, however, you may not think of a specific need, but later something comes to mind. So if you have a list of specific tasks available, caring people can select the ways they want to help.

When helping Barbara recuperate, I made a list of a number of helpful tasks, such as organizing family pictures to put inside existing frames and hanging items on walls. In fact, when Charles arrived with Mary Ruth, he was the only one tall enough (at least ten feet tall, I'm sure!) to drive the nail above the doorway to display a patriotic plaque—something Barbara couldn't do postsurgery.

Each to-do task can be listed on a separate index card and placed in a convenient tray. Then when someone offers to help, let them choose from the list of needs and allow them to take the card to serve as a tangible reminder.

SOME SUGGESTIONS:
- Pick up medications.
- Shop for groceries.
- Mail packages, purchase stamps.
- Get or return library books or videos.
- Take patient for a haircut.
- Provide massage/manicure/pedicure.
- Take care of car: fuel, fluids, tires, other maintenance (oil change, tune-up, car wash).
- Perform home repair/car repair.
- Walk the dog, take pets to vet/groomer.
- Water grass/plants/flowers.
- Mow lawn/rake leaves/shovel snow.
- Take out trash/recycle items.
- Vacuum, dust, clean mirrors.
- Change sheets, do laundry, iron.
- Host a party in the patient's house if appropriate; stay and clean up afterward.
- Take photos of an event.
- Make a scrapbook.

- Address thank-you notes, birthday/Christmas cards.
- Write checks to pay bills, balance checkbook.
- Type and distribute a phone tree, e-mail, or prayer list.
- Sort mail and e-mail.

Last but not least on this list proved to be meaningful to my sister Swanee when Charles was battling cancer: stay with the patient for an extended visit so the caregiver (Swanee) could attend to errands, meetings, or personal needs.

To provide needed relief for Swanee, nine days before Charles died, I spent an hour and a half alone talking with him. In fact, I read many pages of *this very book* to him—and he loved it! What a high privilege to seek to meet both of their needs at the same time.

> *"Share with God's people who are in need."*
> ROMANS 12:13

Placemat of special people made by Cheryl

ACCOMPANY YOUR LOVED ONE
TO CHEMO

After several months of chemotherapy, I called my dear friend who had been fighting cancer for several years. "Sue, please forgive me for being so insensitive." "There's nothing you've done to forgive," she responded.

"Oh yes, there is." I protested. "Tell me, what could I have done for you that would have been truly meaningful?"

"Oh June, you didn't need to do anything."

"No, Sue. Tell me. What would have really been meaningful?"

Again she deflected my questions. "I didn't want to take you away from the important work you are doing," she assured me.

"No, I really want to know," I insisted.

"Well . . ." she hesitated, then softly answered, "I wish you had come with me just once for chemotherapy."

Of course! How easy that would have been. But I didn't know. Yet at the same time, I realize how comforting it was for me to have understanding friends and family during those times of my own treatment. Sue's words helped me to have focus.

A few weeks later, another friend was scheduled for her first chemo treatment. I'll never forget the look of surprise and joy on Muriel's face when I walked in and sat with her for an hour as she embarked on her new, uncertain journey. If I had not traveled this same path, I wouldn't have known how to be sensitive to her need.

I can sincerely say that what others have looked upon as bad has been truly used for good in my life. And I pray that God will continue to use my chemo experience to help me to be sensitive and to reach out to the needs of others.

My friend Sue has since gone home to be with the Lord, and although I miss her terribly at times, I am grateful that her long, hard-fought battle with cancer is over and that she is now literally walking with her Lord and enjoying the place He had prepared specifically for her. I am also grateful that her life is still impacting my life and the lives of others.

Sue was one of my "fun," forever friends. I love to think of her with her head back, eyes sparkling, and peals of laughter coming from her mouth. She was one of God's precious, beautiful blessings. He had a special call on her life, and because of her life He is still working for my good and for the good of others.

> *"We know that in all things God works for the good of those who love him, who have been called according to his purpose."*
> ROMANS 8:28

> *I can sincerely say that what others have looked upon as bad has been truly used for good in my life.*
> JUNE

PART TWO

Help and Hope

Don't Forget about the Children

When a father or mother has a life-threatening illness, often the stress is so great and the grief so deep that children get lost in the shuffle. Because life has taken a dramatic turn for the parents, another adult may need to come alongside to help the children make the turn also.

Perhaps the greatest gift you can give to a parent struggling with a serious illness is choosing to focus on the children: learn their likes and dislikes, notice their needs, and help them face their fears. Consider these possible suggestions:

- When visiting your friend, be a friend to the children. Spend time talking with each child, if possible, one on one. Begin with general questions such as, "What do you like most about school?" "Who is your favorite teacher and why?" "How is this year different from last year?"
- Bring a batch of home-baked cookies for them to put in their lunch boxes or enough for them to share with their friends. Better yet, give the goodies to their mother to give to the children. This helps Mom still feel like a mom!
- Be aware of Christmas and birthday gifts. Ask your friend, "Would you like for me to buy something special for you to give to Jimmy?" If so, buy the gift wrap as well, but let your friend see the gift before it's wrapped.
- Purchase humorous cards, posters, or gifts for your loved one to give. Although this is a heavy time, these fun items allow the sick one to introduce some much-needed levity. Remember, children love to laugh.
- Carry a camera when you visit. Take pictures of the children, both by themselves as well as with their parents. Put exceptional pictures in a frame. Even though most of the attention is on the one who is ill, this special attention lets the kids know that they are still important.
- Volunteer for needed transportation for a child's field trip or a birthday party. Be sure to inquire ahead of time about what the child is to bring.
- After treatments have become routine, offer to take the children to observe a chemo treatment for a little while. Doing so may take away the mystique and answer many questions they may

have about this part of the therapy. It would also allow them to be a part of the process with their family member.

- Take the children to buy school supplies or school clothes or a special outfit for no particular occasion. One grown daughter continues year after year to thank me for taking her (along with her brother and sisters) to buy clothes during a time when their mother was physically incapacitated. I'm still absolutely amazed at the long-term impact this one act of kindness has had through the years.

Amid the maze of emotions, the children need to be assured that they aren't suddenly less loved and that their welfare isn't less important. A parent's severe illness is a clear case of a family in crisis, and you can help the family by focusing on the children. Keeping a child's routine of school, activities, and friends is very helpful to the child.

Will these and other little acts of kindness make any real difference? Yes, beyond a shadow of doubt! The greatest treasures in God's kingdom are built from the smallest acts of kindness toward His little ones. A truly unselfish gift is one that is given to those who cannot return the favor. And, in the eyes of the Lord, any act of kindness toward someone in need is an act of love toward Him. Jesus said, "'I was hungry and you gave Me food; I was thirsty and you gave Me drink; I was a stranger and you took Me in; I was naked and you clothed Me; I was sick and you visited Me.' . . . 'Lord, when did we see You hungry and feed You, or thirsty and give You drink? When did we see You a stranger and take You in, or naked and clothe You?' . . . 'Inasmuch as you did it to one of the least of these My brethren, you did it to Me'" (Matt. 25:35–40 NKJV).

PRACTICE
RANDOM
ACTS
OF
KINDNESS

52

QUESTIONS TO HELP CHILDREN

Preserving life takes precedence over everyone and everything else. But if the real needs of the children are not met, they can feel cut off from their parents, confused about God, and disconnected from the lives they have known. Asking key questions, showing real interest, and talking heart to heart can help turn children in the direction they need to go now and protect them from suffering residual negative side effects in the future.

- "What do you know about Mommy's illness?"
- "Do you know what caused Daddy's cancer?"
- "Do you know that you've not done or said anything that has caused Mommy's sickness?"
- "What would you like to do for Daddy to express your love for him?"
- "Are you afraid you too may become sick?"
- "Are there some questions you have about what the doctors are doing to try to help Mommy get well?"
- "Do you know that it is okay to feel sad or upset because Daddy is so sick and unable to do things with you like he used to?"
- "Would you like to go to the doctor's office with Mommy sometime so you can see what she does down there?"
- "Do you know that there's still no one in the world that Mommy and Daddy love more than you? You will always be special in their hearts."
- "What do you do when you feel sad about Daddy's illness?"
- "Would you like for us to pray together and ask Jesus to take care of Mommy, to comfort and encourage her, and to let her know how much you love her?"
- "Could we pray together and thank Jesus for taking care of you, asking Him to also comfort and encourage you?"
- "Do you know that Mommy and Daddy will always love you and will make sure that you are always taken care of?"
- "What things have changed for you since Mommy has been sick?"
- "What are some things you and I can do to make Daddy feel better?"
- "What do you think about your Mommy's illness?"
- "What are some of the things you think about or worry about?"

- "Do you know about the things your Daddy is doing to try to get better?"
- "Would you like for us to think of some special things you could do for your mother, like reading her favorite Scriptures to her or reading to her from a book that she likes or writing thank-you notes for her?"

Honest discussion in a positive, hopeful way helps dispel children's fears and misconceptions.

"The tongue of the wise brings healing."

PROVERBS 12:18

53

TIPS FOR TEMPORARY TRIALS

No person gives better driving directions than a driver who has already gone where you need to go. Likewise, no person gives better advice on a trial than someone who has persevered in that same type of trial. In the midst of the trials of cancer treatment, the counsel of one who has gone before is an invaluable gift worth its weight in gold. The list below reflects practical wisdom from caring people who preceded me in tackling their trials. "The lips of the wise spread knowledge" (Prov. 15:7).

BEFORE BEGINNING TREATMENTS[20]
- Tell your doctor what medications (prescription and over-the-counter), vitamins, and the like that you are taking and whether you have any allergies. Some medications, herbs, and vitamins can interfere with the effectiveness of treatments.
- Obtain a complete dental/oral checkup. Once you begin chemotherapy, your mouth can become too sensitive and too susceptible to infection for dental work.

BEFORE EACH TREATMENT
- Eat solid food—but only nibble, nibble, nibble on the day of chemo and one to two days afterward so as not to overextend the stomach.

AFTER EACH TREATMENT
- Drink plenty of liquids to flush the chemicals out of your body: water (preferably filtered or spring water), fruit juices, lemonade, ginger ale, and club soda.
- Frozen fruit bars and ice cubes help hydrate your body. Avoid caffeine and alcohol because both cause dehydration.

ACHING BONES/JOINTS
- Be sure to take 400 to 1000 IU daily of Vitamin D and have your blood level checked. Antiestrogen hormone blockers can cause aching bones/joints.
- Nonsteroidal anti-inflammatory drugs can be purchased over the counter and can be helpful in controlling or relieving pain.

- If necessary, take prescription medication for discomfort as your physician recommends.

ANEMIA (LOW RED BLOOD CELL COUNT)

- Eat beets, red meat, liver, and especially green vegetables such as spinach, broccoli, and dark green leafy salads, which are excellent sources of iron. (Avoid iceberg lettuce, which has little nutritional value and is very hard to digest.)
- Some say that one tablespoon daily of unsulfured blackstrap molasses was the answer to their low red blood cell count.
- With the consent of your physician, consider taking nutritional supplements that can help build your blood count. Many physicians know the value of sublingual B_{12} or B_{12} injections.

ANTIOXIDANT FOODS (CANCER FIGHTERS)

- Fruits: Apples, berries, cantaloupe, cherries, grapes, oranges, and plums all help fight cancer. Berries also protect the DNA from damage. Cherries contain *anthocyanins*, powerful antioxidants.
- Nuts: Raw almonds contain laetrile, which is thought by many to be a good cancer fighter.
- Vegetables: The cabbage family, called "cruciferous," contains more cancer-fighting properties than any other group—cabbage, broccoli, brussels sprouts, cauliflower, horseradish, mustard greens, radishes, rutabagas, turnips, and watercress.
- Carrots and carrot juice are a source of *beta carotene*, thought to boost the immune system.
- Green vegetables contain *chlorophyll*, another cancer fighter.
- Mushrooms and legumes (including chick peas, lentils, and red beans) also contain vital nutrients.
- Onions and garlic enhance the immune system. Garlic is a natural antibiotic.

CONSTIPATION

- Eat prunes, bran, wheat, and rye bread, and other fiber products.
- Drink prune juice, water, and other liquids. Hot prune juice is especially helpful.

DIARRHEA[21]

- Limit *high fiber* food or other foods that cause cramps or gas, such as raw fruits and vegetables, caffeine, beans, cabbage,

whole-grain breads, cereals, lactose-based dairy products, sweets, and spicy foods.
- Eat *low fiber* foods like bananas, potatoes, and apricots, which are also high in potassium.
- Over-the-counter, natural, dietary fiber supplements can help stop diarrhea.
- Drink clear liquids, including weak tea, broth, apple juice, and soup to avoid dehydration.
- Electrolytes and hydration lost through diarrhea can be replenished with certain over-the-counter drinks (some are suitable for children). At least one comes as a frozen bar, which provides variety.
- Acidophilus capsules and yogurt with live cultures help replenish the loss of good bacteria.
- Keep an over-the-counter antidiarrheal medication nearby or carry it with you.

DRY/CRACKED SKIN
- Mercury-free fish oil capsules replenish oils throughout the body (up to four capsules a day).
- If you are troubled by dry skin, a good moisturizing cream rich with emollients may give comfort.
- Dry, chapped hands can be helped by liberally applying a therapeutic hand cream and covering the hands with cotton gloves to hold in moisture.

DRY EYES
- Eye drops of saline solution can be carried wherever you go.

ENERGY LOSS
- The two fastest sources of energy are orange juice and honey.
- Since energy begets energy, do some aerobic exercise, such as vigorous walking, swimming, or biking every day (or at least four times a week). Exercise promotes oxygenation of the tissues.

FINGERNAIL SPLITTING
- Biotin supplements can promote strong nails and hair (but check with your doctor before taking).
- Eat Jell-O and other gelatin products.

- Use clear nail strengthener or polish made for brittle nails to help keep the nail intact.
- Avoid polish remover containing acetone or alcohol, which is very drying to nails and skin.

HAIR LOSS (ALOPECIA)[22]

- Patients who are prescribed certain chemotherapy drugs inevitably experience hair loss. Hair releases from the scalp between days fourteen and eighteen. When chemo stops, hair growth starts.
- Initially, hair grows back with a different texture (usually baby fine), a different thickness (usually thinner at first), and a different shape (usually curly). Hair may even grow back a different color. (Blondes, this could be your chance to become brunettes!)
- Hair even grows back at different speeds on different parts of the head (faster in the back, slower in the front). So, be patient, patient, patient. Usually six months after chemotherapy ends, you will have grown about one to two inches of hair. Following chemotherapy, hair takes longer to grow than normal, and it may not return as it once was. (Just make the best of those "bad hair days.")

HOT FLASHES

- Dress in layers.
- Avoid caffeine and alcohol.
- Exercise regularly.
- Be aware that spicy foods can exacerbate hot flashes.

LYMPHEDEMA

- Lymphedema (a condition of excessive swelling) may affect up to 10 percent of those who have axillary lymph nodes removed (see p. 64).
- Lifting or carrying heavy items can cause or increase swelling. Have grocery bags (and purses!) loaded lightly and avoid carrying bags using straps or handles across the forearm.
- Have blood taken, injections given, and blood pressure measured from the unaffected arm and hand.
- Avoid extreme temperature changes (such as very hot or cold water).
- Because cuts and abrasions may lead to infections, which are harder to combat when the lymphatic system is compromised, avoid any type of injury to the hand, arm, or underarm. Use an

electric razor instead of a blade to shave underarms. Wear gloves while gardening to avoid puncture wounds.

- When traveling by airplane, wear a pressure glove and a pressure sleeve to keep swelling to a minimum.
- Gently "massaging" the swollen area as by a certified lymph-edema specialist, and wrapping the hand/arm are very effective at minimizing swelling.

MOUTH DRYNESS[23]

- Sip cool water throughout the day, suck ice chips, and eat frozen fruit bars.
- Suck on sugar-free hard candy or chew sugar-free gum.
- Avoid tobacco and alcoholic drinks, for they cause dryness.
- Moisten food with butter, broth, gravies, and sauces.
- Use lip balm for dry lips.
- Ask your doctor about products that either replace or stimulate your own saliva.

MOUTH SORES (STOMATITIS)[24]

- Avoid acidic foods (tomatoes, citrus fruit, and fruit juice), which can cause mouth and throat irritation. Avoid spices and coarse foods, such as raw vegetables, dry crackers, and granola.
- Eat soft foods that are easy to swallow, such as eggs, cooked cereal, soft fruit (bananas and applesauce), soup, mashed potatoes, cottage cheese, macaroni and cheese, ice cream, custard, and yogurt with live cultures.
- Change the consistency of foods by adding fluids and using soups, sauces, and gravies to make them softer.
- Cut your food into small, bite-sized pieces and chew longer than usual.
- Puree your food or drink liquid food supplements.
- Avoid hot beverages. Cold beverages are soothing to the mouth. Put wet washcloths inside plastic zip bags and keep them in the freezer. Later apply to the sore mouth.
- Brush teeth lightly with an extra soft toothbrush using a fluoride toothpaste containing no abrasives. Avoid using dental floss. (If you feel you must, floss gently with waxed, nonshredding floss.)
- Rinse your mouth gently and frequently with a solution made of 1/2 teaspoon baking soda and 1/2 teaspoon salt in a large glass of warm water, especially after you brush. Follow with a plain water rinse.

- Use only an alcohol-free mouthwash. (Alcohol has a drying effect on the mouth tissues.) Prescription mouthwashes may provide significant relief.
- When taking pills, if normal drinking water feels irritating in your mouth (which it did for me), use lightly salted liquids, such as chicken or beef broth. (As strange as it sounds, sometimes I needed to add a little salt to my drinking water.)
- Acidophilus capsules can have a balancing effect on the bacteria and fungus makeup of the body. (I took four capsules labeled "acidophilus with goat's milk" several times a day. And no, you don't taste the goat's milk—it's inside the capsule! Consult your doctor first.)

NAUSEA[25]

- Eat small, frequent amounts of bland food: dry toast, crackers, gelatin, salty chips, ramen noodle soup, ginger snaps, other ginger products, cold dill or sour pickles, carbonated drinks, high carbohydrate foods, oatmeal, potatoes, rice, wheat toast, spaghetti, macaroni and cheese, and other pasta dishes.
- Avoid fried or high-fat foods and foods with a strong aroma.
- Drink cold water or suck on ice chips between meals.
- Eat a light meal one or two hours before and after your treatment, eating and drinking slowly.
- Prepare for the trip home from the chemo treatments with some very helpful items: a plastic basin or pan for nausea, wet washcloths in plastic zip bags, a roll of paper towels, a box of facial tissues, some crushed ice in a cooler to help with nausea, a cup and a spoon (for eating ice chips), ginger ale, a bottle of water, and a pillow.
- Consult your physician about using suppositories and/or oral medications for nausea, including an antiemetic to prevent nausea prior to treatment.

NOSEBLEEDS

- Mercury-free fish oil capsules replenish oils in the tissues of your skin.
- Sleep with a cool mist humidifier (not warm) close to your bed.
- Cold washcloths to the nose will help stop the bleeding.

PLATELET LOSS

- Platelets are those particles that plug up little holes in our blood systems so that we don't ooze blood all the time. Excessive loss of platelets can lead to excessive bleeding or "free bleeding." Expect to bruise easily until the platelet count is restored to your normal range.
- Although rare, in order to protect yourself from internal bleeding, you may need one or more platelet transfusions to replace this needed element in your blood. (I had two transfusions.)
- Protect yourself from any possible skin cuts, scrapes, or pricks because external bleeding may be difficult to stop. Avoid activities with sharp objects like needles, razors, knives, and thorny plants.
- If you have a head cold or a chest cold, blow your nose gently using a soft tissue.
- Wear long sleeves to help protect the skin.
- Do not take pain relievers (aspirin, ibuprofen, etc.) without first consulting your doctor. These medications can weaken the platelets and cause excessive bleeding.

RED BLOOD CELL COUNT LOSS

- You may develop anemia during chemotherapy. Symptoms include fatigue, shortness of breath, and dizziness. Your doctor can prescribe something that will help rebuild your blood count or may recommend a red blood cell transfusion and thus relieve the uncomfortable symptoms.

SWELLING

- Avoid salty foods.
- Keep legs and feet elevated above your heart when sitting and, if necessary, when sleeping.
- For excessive swelling of the legs, ask your physician about wearing compression hose.
- Some prescription diuretics are potassium depleting while others are not. Your doctor may decide it is necessary for you to take a potassium supplement in order to keep the electrolytes in your heart functioning properly.

TOENAIL FUNGUS AND DETACHING

- Trim each affected toenail to conform to the toe, and then forget about it. Following chemotherapy, toenails usually grow back.

- Soak feet in Epsom salts if nails loosen or drain.
- Be patient—regrowth will take a number of months.

WEIGHT GAIN

- Know that gaining weight is temporary because fluid buildup is temporary. Your metabolism may also be "out of commission" because of chemo.
- Losing weight will be easier after chemo when steroids are no longer needed as part of the chemotherapy treatment. Continue to walk briskly or do any other aerobic exercises to increase your metabolism.

WHITE CELL COUNT LOSS (LEUKOPENIA)

- Your doctor may treat you with specific medications for a loss of white cells in the blood. Repeated injections help rebuild bone marrow, which is essential because bone marrow produces the white cells necessary to fight infection. If the white blood cell count drops excessively low, you may need to be hospitalized and given antibiotics until the medication takes effect. Call your doctor when symptoms occur. Many side effects can be treated; however, not seeking help immediately can allow them to worsen. You must keep in mind that you're not "bothering" the doctor or nurse! Remember, *if you have a temperature of 100.5 degrees or greater, call your doctor or nurse, day or night!*

2002 Baylor Health Circle of Care Award
Dr. Ronald Jones, June, and Gloria Campos

DISCOVER THE IMPORTANT
DON'TS

As I progressed through my cancer treatment, I developed an acute awareness of "the little things"—like every little thing I put in my mouth! Suddenly everything became suspect as I sought to be wise and cancer minded in all I ate, even down to the vitamins I took daily. And if I even *thought about* cheating, Kay or one of my other watchdog friends was looking over my shoulder to keep me on the straight and narrow. I quickly learned some valuable "don'ts" for anyone determined to develop new healthy habits in the midst of the cancer ordeal.

DON'T BE IGNORANT ABOUT ANTIOXIDANTS

This was one of my biggest surprises. At the onset of the chemotherapy treatments, my oncologist, Dr. Joyce O'Shaughnessy, asked me to bring a list of all vitamins and medications I was currently taking. She also wanted me to consult with her before I took anything that caring people would send or suggest, even if the supplements are generally thought to be safe and effective for healthy people.

Imagine my surprise when Dr. O. immediately—and permanently—deleted from my stash of pills the daily dose of 1000 mg of time-release vitamin C that I had taken for years. Immediately I asked, "Why should I eliminate this vitamin, which is known for its antioxidant, cell protection effects?" She explained that current research reveals that vitamin C and other antioxidants such as beta carotene may unfortunately protect the bad cancer cells from the *good* killing effects of chemotherapy and radiation therapy. Because of this uncertainty, many oncologists recommend avoiding supplemental vitamin C. A normal diet and a regular multivitamin should be enough.

DON'T ASSUME THAT SOY MILK IS OKAY

Consult your doctor before consuming soy products on a regular basis. Researchers continue to explore whether the estrogen in soy might either stimulate breast cancer or interfere with the benefit of one of the hormone blocker prescriptions if the cancer is "estrogen-receptor positive." Most oncologists do not recommend taking supplements high in soy with estrogen-receptor positive cancer.

DON'T CONSUME ALCOHOL

The American Cancer Society reports that having two to five drinks a day increases the risk of cancer recurring by 50 percent. "Alcohol consumption is an established cause of cancers of the mouth, pharynx, larynx, esophagus, liver, and breast. For each of these cancers, risk increases substantially with intake of more than two drinks per day. Regular consumption of even a few drinks per week has been associated with an increased risk of breast cancer in women."[26]

DON'T BE UNINFORMED ABOUT WEIGHT GAIN, INSULIN, AND CANCER RECURRENCE

Although there is no clear evidence that sugar itself promotes cancer growth, what is increasingly clear is that steady weight gain and lack of exercise increase insulin levels and that this increases the risk of cancer recurrence. Attaining and maintaining a healthy weight, a slow, steady weight loss, and exercise all effectively lower insulin levels.

DON'T FORGET ABOUT EXERCISE

Walking briskly three hours a week reduces the risk of dying of breast cancer *and* substantially reduces the side effects of chemotherapy and radiation therapy.

DON'T BE UNINFORMED ABOUT HRT

Hormone Replacement Therapy (HRT) has its definite advantages, most notably protection against osteoporosis, vaginal dryness, and relief from hot flashes. However, doctors usually counsel individuals to weigh the benefits of hormone replacement (estrogen, progestin) against the risks of developing cancer. If hormones are used, they usually recommend the lowest dose for the shortest possible time to achieve the desired goals.[27]

BOTTOM LINE

Talk to the doctor about the don'ts. As you read, study, share information with one another, and talk with your doctors, you will know how to be prudent and avoid the danger zones. The Bible gives this caution: "The prudent see danger and take refuge, but the simple keep going and suffer for it" (Prov. 27:12).

> June ~ with love + prayers
>
> For God hath not given us the spirit of fear ~ but of power and of ~love~ and of a ~sound mind~ ~
>
> ~ II Timothy Ch. 1 ~
>
> your sister ~ Helen

WHAT CANCER CANNOT DO

What Cancer Cannot Do

    It cannot lessen love.

    It cannot fracture faith.

    It cannot hinder hope.

    It cannot prevent peace.

    It cannot crush confidence.

    It cannot kill friendship.

    It cannot keep out memories.

    It cannot corrode courage.

    It cannot shatter the soul.

    It cannot quench the spirit.

    It cannot stop resurrection power.

    It cannot erode eternal life.

AUTHOR UNKNOWN
ADAPTED BY JUNE HUNT

FOR THOSE WHO NEED
SPIRITUAL HEALING

"You don't know?" my niece asked.

"Know what?" I responded.

"Uncle Charles was just diagnosed with brain cancer."

"What!" I exclaimed.

"They think it's the same kind of cancer that Senator Ted Kennedy has—a *glioma* [*glioblastoma*]." Kimberly continued, "He's having surgery tomorrow."

WHEN CRISIS HITS

My sister's e-mail informing the family went out Saturday. This was Sunday—surgery was Monday. I asked myself, *What should I do? Should I fly to Boston right now?* After teaching all day Saturday and losing much sleep, I felt exhausted and I knew I had a packed schedule the next week. However, I also knew: there are very few crisis times in a person's life. This was, indeed, a crisis—a monumental crisis!

My personal belief is: *When a crisis hits—reach out, call, go!* So within fifteen minutes, I was packed and on my way to the airport. Then after a four–hour flight, when I walked into his hospital room, my sister and brother-in-law were stunned. Looking back, I've never made a more "right" decision—simply to *go.* And yes, the diagnosis was a *glioma*—which, in spite of surgery, meant a typical prognosis of twelve or fourteen months to live . . . maybe a little more.

During that year, I tried to think of a variety of creative ways to reach out—fun cards, personalized poems, cashmere socks ("footsies for your tootsies"), and a blanket that he eventually *insisted on* sleeping under every night. And since he didn't have a sister (only three brothers), I designed an official-looking, yet humorous adoption certificate. From then on he called me "Sister June," and with a lilt in my voice, I called him "Brother Charles."

Meanwhile, as the founder and conductor of the Boston Landmarks Orchestra, Charles maintained a vigorous schedule of performances. That year, I attended several of his concerts because for a conductor, the most meaningful "gift" you can give is just show-ing up! Eventually, the time came when I knew I was flying in for his personal finale—his own final concert. By this time, Charles could only conduct the opening number and the encore—a guest conductor did the rest. Nevertheless, I came to support him emotionally and, if the opportunity was available, to reach out to him *spiritually* since I knew he had never acknowledged any belief in God.

On a Wednesday evening, one year following his first surgery, I felt so grateful that I could enjoy—with eight thousand other fans—the season finale, which concluded with the rip-roaring, toe-tapping, flag-waving "Stars and Stripes Forever." What a huge success! And, under-standably, the following day (Thursday), Charles was physically spent.

Since my plane was scheduled to leave Friday afternoon, I sim-ply prayed for the privilege—if it was God's will—of presenting to Charles how to know God and have eternal life. As Friday morning came and went, I began to think this special one-on-one time wasn't meant to be. Then, at 1:00 p.m., my sister Swanee said, "Now would be a perfect time for you and Charles to visit."

APPEALING TO AN ATHEIST

After entering his bedroom and sitting down with him, I explained that I had decided to dedicate this cancer book to him. He seemed so genuinely pleased. Knowing Charles had grown up in a home that held an atheistic worldview, I asked a series of questions and received his predictable answers:

- "Am I correct that you consider yourself an atheist?" (*Yes*, he answered.)
- "Do you consider yourself open minded or closed minded?" (*Open minded.*) "That's good."
- "Do you consider yourself intellectually honest?" (*I would say so.*) "I would agree with you."
- "Do you consider yourself a seeker of truth?" (*Yes, yes.*) "Excel-lent!"

On a large piece of paper, I drew a very large circle, and said to Charles, "This circle represents all the knowledge in the world. For example, all scientific formulas, all historical facts, all math equations, all languages, cultures, and literature, all music, art, technology, and medicine. Of all the knowledge in the world, what amount do you think you possess? Simply draw a circle inside the large circle that represents all of *your* knowledge."

ALL KNOWLEDGE   all **your** knowledge

Charles drew a small circle about the size of a pencil eraser. We continued . . .

- "You said you are open minded. Is that correct?" (*Yes.*)
- "And you said you are intellectually honest—correct?" (*Yes.*)
- "Then is it just *possible* God could exist outside your small circle of knowledge?" (Pause—*I would have to say yes.*)
- "Since you admit you don't know everything there is to know and you agree that God could exist outside your circle of knowledge, that means you really aren't an atheist, you're an *agnostic*. You just *don't know* if God exists, correct?" (*That's true.*)
- "Well, realize being an agnostic cannot be the ultimate long-term position to hold because there either *is a God* or there *isn't a God*. Do you agree?" (*Yes.*)
- "Since you said you are a *seeker of truth*, would you be willing to hear how others have entered into a relationship with God?" (*Yes, I would.*) Then I mentioned the names of several people whom Charles personally knew and respected who were authentic Christians and who boldly declare they know God personally. Immediately, he commented on how each one had touched his life in a meaningful way.

As we talked for close to an hour, Charles paid rapt attention to every word—totally engaged. At that point, I picked up the earlier, in-house edition of this book, showed him the different sections, and literally began reading every word in the last chapter to guide our conversation. I explained that every person has a tangible body and, based on the Bible, an intangible spirit. Our spirit is eternal—it will last forever. Our present body is temporal—it's destined to die, but the spirit will exist either forever with God or forever away from God. (The first is called "spiritual life." The second, "spiritual death.") I said to Charles, "The reason I'm sharing this with you is because I love you. The bottom line is: *Eternity is too long to be wrong*." And then I went on to explain . . .

HOW TO HAVE SPIRITUAL LIFE

Recognize there is a problem.

Consider this, if your body is terminally ill because of cancer, what would happen if a healthy man could and would exchange his healthy body for your cancerous body? Physically, he would die and you would live! Likewise, your spirit is "terminally ill" due to being imperfect (what the Bible calls "sin"). The Bible says, "Anyone . . . who knows the good he ought to do and doesn't do it, sins,"[28] and also, "The soul who sins is the one who will die."[29] Well, the truth is, we've all sinned.[30]

And as a result, we've got a problem! Scripture says, "Your iniquities [sins] have separated you from your God."[31] In reality, we've all chosen wrong—we've all been separated. But, if we don't want to be separated, yet can't change the fact that we've sinned, we're stuck with a most difficult dilemma.

God took the initiative to solve the problem.

You know you're not perfect—but what would happen if a perfect man could and would exchange his perfection for your imperfection? Spiritually, he would die and you would live. God the Father sent His perfect Son, Jesus, to pay the penalty for your sins. He died in your place and then rose again so that you could receive His full forgiveness and live forever with God. The Bible explains, "God demonstrates his own love for us in this: While we were still sinners, Christ died for us."[32] He willingly offers you this great exchange—His death for your life.

You have a part in the solution—a decision to make.

In order to receive this forgiveness, you must humble your heart, be willing to confess your sins, and turn from them. The Bible reveals, "If we confess our sins, he is faithful and just and will forgive us our sins and purify us from all unrighteousness."[33] When you receive

Jesus as your personal Lord and Savior—giving Him control of your life—He forgives all of your sins and gives you eternal life. The Bible declares this good news: "God so loved the world that he gave his one and only Son, that whoever believes in him shall not perish but have eternal life."[34]

God offers you a great gift.
Assume you desperately need cancer medication that your money can't buy. Then, all of a sudden, you hear that a gift has been offered to you—not aspirin, not cough medicine, but the *only* medicine that could cure your cancer. For the medicine to be effective, you need to believe it and receive it—and take it into you.

Salvation is like that. You need to believe what God says is true and receive God's gift to you by faith and apply it to your life. God says that your salvation is based on your faith in Christ—entrusting your life to Jesus Christ alone. Jesus said, "I am the way and the truth and the life. No one comes to the Father except through me."[35]

Not telling a dying person how to receive spiritual life—how to be saved—would be as unthinkable as discovering the cure for cancer, yet being unwilling to share it! Close to the end of our conversation, Charles was silent for a moment, then intently looked at me and said, "June, I have never heard this before!" Imagine—my brilliant "adopted brother"—despite all of his world travels and associations—had never heard the most wonderful, life-changing news ever told! How grateful I was that God had given me the words to share and Charles the ears to hear.

At that point, I took his hand and prayed with Charles, basically asking that God would guard his mind from error and confirm only truth to his heart. When I finished praying, he didn't release his grip, but instead with bowed head prayed, "And Whoever is up there, thank you for sending June to me." How unexpected!

Before I left, I put a bookmark in the chapter I had just read, saying, "Charles, if you'd like to review much of what we talked about, it's right here." He thanked me profusely, and I said goodbye, knowing this would be the last time I would see my "Brother Charles" here on earth. Before leaving for the airport, I sought to relay to my sister everything we talked about, including the prayer he prayed. Clearly surprised, Swanee said, "Well, that's a first—he's never said a prayer before in his life!"

After our time together, I returned to Dallas. Nine days later, my Brother Charles died and I flew back to Boston to sing at his memorial service. I felt so honored that I could honor him in his language—the language of music.

Shortly after I returned home, I learned that he had told numerous people about our conversation. Swanee shared these tender words with me, "I'm convinced that Charles found God." I'm thankful that I can trust God with matters beyond my knowledge and control, thankful that I can trust Him with those I love. I am able to say, "It is well with my soul." And so it has been to this very day. And so it will be throughout the rest of this life and the life to come.

The Prayer for Spiritual Life

If you want to become spiritually alive—spiritually whole—you can receive this new life now by sincerely praying this prayer:

> God, I admit that I'm not perfect and that I have sinned.
> Many times, I have gone my own way instead of Your way.
> Please forgive me for all of my sins.
> Thank You, Jesus, for dying on the cross
> to pay the penalty for my sins.
> Come into my life to be my Lord and Savior.
> Take control of my life and
> make me the person You want me to be.
> Thank You, Jesus, for what You will do
> in me, to me, and through me.
> In Your holy name, I pray. Amen.

From the concert
of life nobody
gets a program

If you sincerely prayed this prayer,
look what God promises you!

*"I tell you the truth, whoever hears my word and
believes him who sent me has eternal life and will not be condemned;
he has crossed over from death to life."*
JOHN 5:24

What Did We Miss?

Do you have a favorite, practical caregiving tip that isn't found in *Caring for a Loved One with Cancer*? Please send it to me via e-mail to cancertips@hopefortheheart.org or write to:

Hope For The Heart
ATTN: Cancer Tips
2001 W. Plano Pkwy.
Suite 1000
Plano, TX 75075

Name: _____

Phone: _____

E-mail: _____

Caregiving Tip: _____

Thank you for letting us learn from you. We seek to provide the best, most useful information to caregivers around the world!

Yours in the Lord's hope,
June Hunt

About the Author

June Hunt is an author, singer, speaker, and founder of HOPE FOR THE HEART, a worldwide biblical counseling ministry featuring the award-winning radio broadcast by the same name heard daily across America. In addition, *HOPE IN THE NIGHT* is June's live two-hour call-in counseling program that helps people untie their tangled problems with *biblical hope and practical help*. HOPE FOR THE HEART'S radio broadcasts air on approximately five hundred radio outlets worldwide.

Early family pain was the catalyst that shaped June's compassionate heart. Later, as a youth director for more than six hundred teenagers, she became aware of the need for sound biblical counseling. Her work with young people and their parents led June to a life commitment of providing *God's Truth for Today's Problems*.

After years of teaching and research, June began developing scripturally based counseling tools called *Biblical Counseling Keys*, which address definitions, characteristics, causes, and solutions for one hundred topics (such as marriage and parenting, anger and abuse, guilt and grief). Recently these individual topics were compiled to create the landmark *Biblical Counseling Library*.

The *Counseling Keys* have become the foundation for HOPE FOR THE HEART'S *Hope Biblical Counseling Institute*, initiated by the Criswell College in 2002. Each monthly conference in the Dallas-based *Institute* provides training to help spiritual leaders, counselors, and other caring Christians meet the very real needs of others.

June has served as a guest professor at colleges and seminaries both nationally and internationally, teaching on topics such as crisis counseling, child abuse, wife abuse, forgiveness, singleness, and self-worth. Her works are currently available in more than sixty countries on six continents, and in twenty-four languages, including Russian, Romanian, Ukrainian, Spanish, Portuguese, German, Mandarin, Korean, Japanese, and Arabic.

She is the author of *Hope for Your Heart, How to Forgive . . . When You Don't Feel Like It, Seeing Yourself Through God's Eyes, Bonding with Your Teen through Boundaries, How to Rise Above Abuse, Counseling Through Your Bible Handbook, How to*

Handle Your Emotions, Keeping Your Cool . . . When Your Anger Is Hot!, How to Defeat Harmful Habits, and more than forty topical HopeBooks. June is also a contributor to the *Soul Care Bible* and the *Women's Devotional Bible.*

An accomplished musician, June has been a guest on numerous national television and radio programs, including the NBC *Today* show. She has toured overseas with the USO and has been a guest soloist at Billy Graham crusades. Five recordings—*Songs of Surrender, Hymns of Hope, The Whisper of My Heart, The Shelter Under His Wings,* and *The Hope of Christmas*—all reflect her heart of hope.

Learn more about June and HOPE FOR THE HEART at . . .

www.HopeForTheHeart.org
2001 W. Plano Parkway, Suite 1000
Plano, TX 75075
1-800-488-HOPE (4673)

American Cancer Society and National Comprehensive Cancer Network. www.cancer.org.

American Cancer Society. *Breast Cancer: Treatment Guidelines for Patients.* Version 5, July 2003. Atlanta, GA: American Cancer Society, 2003.

———. *Cancer Facts and Figures 2005.* Atlanta, GA: American Cancer Society, 2005.

———. "Detailed Guide: Breast Cancer: What are the Risk Factors for Breast Cancer?" 2004. American Cancer Society. http://www.cancer.org/ docroot/CRI/content/CRI_2_4_2X_What_are_the_risk_factors_for_ breast_cancer_5.asp?sitearea=.

Cooke, Joanna. "Lymphedema after Breast Cancer." Breast Cancer Action Kingston: 2002. http://www.bcakingston.org/lymphedema.html.

Department of Health and Human Services, National Institutes of Health. www.nih.gov.

Hunt, June. *Counseling Through Your Bible Handbook: Providing Biblical Hope and Practical Help for 50 Everyday Problems.* Eugene, OR: Harvest House, 2008.

———. *Hope for Your Heart: Finding Strength in Life's Storms.* Wheaton, IL: Crossway, 2011.

———. *How to Forgive . . . When You Don't Feel Like It.* Eugene, OR: Harvest House, 2007.

———. *How to Handle Your Emotions: Anger, Depression, Fear, Grief, Rejection, Self-Worth.* Eugene, OR: Harvest House, 2008.

———. *How to Rise Above Abuse: Victory for Victims of Five Types of Abuse.* Eugene, OR: Harvest House, 2010.

———. *Keeping Your Cool . . . When Your Anger Is Hot! Practical Steps to Temper Fiery Emotions.* Eugene, OR: Harvest House, 2009.

———. *Seeing Yourself through God's Eyes: A 31-Day Devotional Guide.* Eugene, OR: Harvest House, 2008.

LaTour, Kathy. *The Breast Cancer Companion: From Diagnosis Through Treatment to Recovery: Everything You Need to Know for Every Step Along the Way.* New York: Avon, 1993.

Love, Susan with Karen Lindsey. *Dr. Susan Love's Breast Book.* Illustrated by Marcia Williams. 3rd ed. Cambridge: Perseus, 2000.

National Cancer Institute. *Radiation Therapy and You: A Guide to Self-help during Cancer Treatment.* Bethesda, MD: National Cancer Institute, 2003.

Quillin, Patrick with Noreen Quillin. *Beating Cancer with Nutrition.* Rev. ed. Carlsbad, CA: Nutrition Times, 2001.

Retsky, Michael. "Cancer Growth: Implications for Medicine and Malpractice." Technical Assistance Bureau, Inc. http://www.tabexperts.com /CancerGrowth.htm.

NOTES

1. Boston Landmarks Orchestra, "Charles Ausbacher: A Remembrance http://www.landmarksorchestra.org/index.php/charles_ansbacher.html.

2. Ibid.

3. Ibid.

4. Ps. 139:16.

5. See also June Hunt, *Hope for Your Heart: Finding Strength in Life's Storms* (Wheaton, IL: Crossway, 2011), p. 70. [chapter 4].

6. Luke 22:42 KJV.

7. Used by permission.

8. American Cancer Society, *Cancer Facts and Figures 2005* (Atlanta, GA: American Cancer Society, 2005), 1.

9. Michael Retsky, "Cancer Growth: Implications for Medicine and Malpractice," Technical Assistance Bureau, Inc., http://www.tabexperts.com/CancerGrowth.htm>.

10. For breast cancer tumor classifications, see American Cancer Society and National Comprehensive Cancer Network, *Breast Cancer: Treatment Guidelines for Patients,* version 5, July 2003 (Atlanta, GA: American Cancer Society, 2003), 13.

11. For cancer stages, see American Cancer Society and National Comprehensive Cancer Network, *Breast Cancer: Treatment Guidelines for Patients,* 14.

12. American Cancer Society, *Cancer Facts and Figures 2005,* 9.

13. For the chemotherapy process, see American Cancer Society and National Comprehensive Cancer Network, *Breast Cancer: Treatment Guidelines for Patients,* 19–25.

14. For the radiation therapy process, see Ibid., 17–18; National Institutes of Health Department of Health and Human Services, National Cancer Institute, *Radiation Therapy and You: A Guide to Self-Help during Cancer Treatment* (Bethesda, MD: National Cancer Institute, 2003), 5.

15. For the hormone therapy process, see American Cancer Society and National Comprehensive Cancer Network, *Breast Cancer: Treatment Guidelines for Patients,* 21.

16. Brent Ray, "The Learning Curve." CaringBridge Journal Entry, May 15, 2001, http://www.caringbridge.org/visit/elaineray/journal/3.

17. Matt. 10:30.

18. Used by permission.

19. Joanna Cooke, "Lymphedema after Breast Cancer," 2002, Breast Cancer Action Kingston <http://www.bcakingston.org/lymphedema.html>.

20. For information regarding beginning your treatment, see National Institutes of Health Department of Health and Human Services, National Cancer Institute, *Radiation Therapy and You: A Guide to Self-Help during Cancer Treatment,* 18, 36.

21. For information regarding avoiding diarrhea with radiation therapy, see Ibid., 42.

22. For information regarding hair loss and radiation therapy, see Ibid., 31.

23. For information regarding mouth dryness and radiation therapy, see Ibid., 38.

24. For information regarding mouth sores and radiation therapy, see Ibid., 36–37.

25. For information regarding nausea and radiation therapy, see Ibid., 41.

26. American Cancer Society, *Cancer Facts and Figures 2005* (Atlanta, GA: American Cancer Society, 2005), 46.

27. *Hormone Replacement Therapy and Breast Cancer Relapse.* February 5, 2004. National Cancer Institute. http://www.cancer.gov/clinicaltrials/results/hrt-and-breast-cancer0204.

28. James 4:17.
29. Ezek. 18:4.
30. Rom. 3:23.
31. Isa. 59:2.
32. Rom. 5:8.
33. 1 John 1:9.
34. John 3:16.
35. John 14:6.

General Index

Jots for the Journey

Jots for the Journey

Jots for the Journey

Jots for the Journey